AN A TO Z OF

NEAR-DEATH ADVENTURES

Brian Hogan

ASTEROIDEA BOOKS
FAYETTEVILLE, ARKANSAS

Brian Hogan / Asteroidea Books
2322 N. Hummingbird Ln.
Fayetteville, AR 72703
(707) 702–1476   info@AsteroideaBooks.com
Web Home: AsteroideaBooks.com

Brian and Louise Hogan are available for speaking in conferences, classes, and other events. For bookings, please use contact information above.

Ordering Information: Quantity sales. Special discounts are available on quantity purchases by corporations, associations, and others. For details, contact the Special Sales Department at the address above.

All stories are non-fiction. For security and protection, names in *J is for Jerk*, *X is for Xenophobia* and *Z is for Zealots* have been changed.

Photos are property of the author, used with permission, or Public Domain.

Scripture taken from THE HOLY BIBLE, NEW INTERNATIONAL VERSION®, NIV® Copyright © 1973, 1978, 1984, 2011 by Biblica, Inc.® Used by permission. All rights reserved worldwide.

Scripture taken from The Message.(MSG) Copyright © 1993, 1994, 1995, 1996, 2000, 2001, 2002. Used by permission of NavPress Publishing Group.

All quotes from *The Princess Bride* are from the Rob Reiner film ©1987, Twentieth Century Fox, not the incredibly similar William Goldman novel.

An A to Z of Near-Death Adventures/Brian Hogan—2nd edition
ISBN 978-0-9799056-7-4

To Louise

Who had to live through so many of my brushes with death and stayed around these past thirty years anyway. I cannot imagine anyone I would rather have peregrinating alongside me.

This book would never have made it to press without your loving and gently persistent encouragement to write and your willingness to endure my long hours of intimacy with the keyboard.

I thank God every day for your absolutely unpredictable response to my impulsively blurted out-of-the-blue query: "When are you going to marry me?" Your reply was a miracle that changed my life: "So when are you going to ask?"

Three decades on I'd do it all again.

*When snatched from the jaws of death,
tooth marks are to be expected.*

—Hal Story

To die will be an awfully big adventure.

—Peter Pan

*. . . the devil . . . was a murderer from the
beginning. . .*

—Jesus (John 8:44)

Table of Adventures

Preface

Life should not be a journey to the grave with the intention of arriving safely in a pretty and well preserved body, but rather to skid in broadside in a cloud of smoke, thoroughly used up, totally worn out, and loudly proclaiming "Wow! What a Ride!"

—Hunter S. Thompson

About four years ago, I awoke in the very early hours of the morning, my mind flooded with remembered instances of extreme danger and narrow escapes. The more I tried to stop thinking and return to sleep, the more stories thrust themselves into my consciousness. Finally, just to clear my mind of this sudden obsession, I got up and typed a list into my laptop. With hardly a pause, I managed to remember thirty-four times in my life where I might have died. Satisfied that I'd cleared my mind, I went back to bed and slept for several hours.

At breakfast, I mentioned the nocturnal thought barrage and the resulting inventory to my wife, Louise. She always takes my dreams and things like this far more seriously than I do. In fact, I keep my weirdest dreams to myself, afraid of what her interpretation may say about me. At any rate, true to form, Louise told me she felt like this was important and from the Holy Spirit. She wanted to see the listing I'd made, and after hearing all the things I'd remembered, a number of which were new to her, she urged me to spend some time praying and considering what it all might mean.

I wasn't anxious to do this. A massive listing of near-death experiences seemed a bit negative and morbid, and it is just not like me to dwell on these kinds of memories. However, I love and respect my wife. I know that she is more spiritually sensitive than me, so I sat there pondering my listing. I actually thought of a few more stories to add to the bottom of the growing catalogue of disasters. I asked God what this was all about. When no answer came (and I mean *came right away*—I like my results immediate and dramatic), I began to play with the word processor file I had typed the list into, adding a title: *Near-Death Adventures*, then tweaking the formatting, picking a font (Chiller seemed appropriate), numbering the list (which I began to realize comprised a bunch of short story titles), etc. Suddenly, the idea to sort the titles alphabetically came to me. I had to search Word's Help to remind myself how to do this automatically. Undoing the numbering, I selected all thirty-seven titles. As I hit the button to *Sort: A–Z*, I felt a strange thrill run though me. There was something important in all this.

Before me was a list that covered almost every letter of the alphabet. A number of letters had several candidates, and a few had none (Q, X, and Z, if I remember correctly). All at once my spine tingled, and I felt completely drawn in. I didn't know why. I spent the next couple of hours working over that document. I reworded many of the story titles and found ways to make them sort more evenly. I managed to find topics that worked for my missing letters. I decided to cull the list down to just twenty-six titles, one for each letter of the alphabet, and retitled my file *An A to Z of Near-Death Adventures*. The stories that didn't make the cut went down to the bottom in a category entitled *Extras*. I then realized there were a number of stories that grouped naturally together under a single word. The list included three times I'd been poisoned (another would come as I was writing this book!), four stories of vehicle peril, two featuring demonic attack, and several about becoming swept up into foreign political unrest. I decided I would cut all my titles down to as close to one word as possible—then use that one word in an alphabetical list of titles: *C is for Cliff, P is for Poison,* etc. I reworked the entire Table of Contents, and by the time I'd finished, I knew I was supposed to record these true-life tales and author a second book. (My first book, *There's a Sheep in my Bathtub: Birth of a Mongolian Church Planting Movement* had been published two years previously.) This collection of stories was to be the account of a concerted lifelong contract by the Prince of Darkness on my life and calling and a glory-filled extravaganza of Divine rescues. I had my answer from God.

Despite the excitement and momentum, I found actually starting the writing to be daunting. A book seems impossible when it is just a blank screen glowing in front of the author's face. This book was to remain just a Table of Contents for almost two years. Finally, I was so frustrated at my complete lack of progress on what I knew to be an assignment from the Father, I decided to force myself to write something, even if it was fit only for deletion. I'd told my mother and aunt one of the stories orally while Mom was in the hospital dying from cancer in July 2011. I'd recorded it and saved the file for transcription. Desperate to get something on paper, I found the recording and hit play, ready to type the words I had spoken. It was almost soundless! Something had been wrong in the microphone settings and I could barely discern a faint murmur. Completely discouraged, I decided to wait for another day and start from scratch. Later that week I was heading into a busy travel season—leaving for three weeks in South Africa to train church planters around Cape Town. I never get anything accomplished on my various projects while I am on the road. Over the years I have come to accept this and have quit lying to myself that I will accomplish a given to-do list on the plane or in my hotel room. (It just occurred to me that I am writing this in my room at the *University of the Nations* in Kona, Hawaii! I am actually getting something done on a trip. Maybe growth and change are even possible at fifty-two years of age!) So, although I shared my vision and title list with a number of folks, I didn't write a single story for three months. I came home from South Africa to a brewing family crisis involving my teen son, Peter, and I shoved the book project even farther into the background.

On November 1st, 2012, I had an inspiration. I formed a private group on Facebook called *Brian Hogan's An A to Z of Near-Death Adventures (the Author's Salon)* with this *About* tag: "A group to read the rough drafts of my 26 chapters as I post them. Feedback welcome." I then sent the following invitation to Facebook friends, only those I actually knew in person, to participate:

An Invitation to be a part of an author's creative process.

I have been wanting to write a book of true life stories for a couple of years now, but have lacked the discipline and accountability to just put words onto "paper" (obviously not tree pulp based—electronic paper). It is titled: An A to Z of Near-Death Adventures (or 26 Ways the Devil Tried to Snuff Me). There will be 26 alphabetically titled chapters— each a separate story. I've roughed out the entire thing. I just need to write the stories themselves.

I just had an idea! I've started a closed Facebook Page for a very select group of 26 interested friends only. I will post each story to the page where you can read and critique each installment (do not repost any).

Voila! I hit the enter key and created an accountability group and scored some volunteer editing to boot! Knowing real people were waiting for me to produce had a galvanizing effect on my creative juices. I wrote out and posted the first chapter, *A is for Abandoned,* before I even got up from the desk. My plan was to post a chapter a day, maybe taking off weekends, for one month. I planned to be finished by December 1st. My grand plan worked perfectly for two days.

On the night of November 2nd, as Louise and I sat together quietly honoring what would have been our son Jedidiah's 18th birthday (Jed died at 2 months in Mongolia on Christmas Eve 1994), our lives imploded with the arrival of sheriff's deputies at our front door. They were seeking Peter, Jedidiah's younger brother, for vandalism. Caught in the act, he had evaded capture. His whereabouts were unknown. For the past three months his behavior and attitude had fallen off a cliff, and though he angrily denied it, I was convinced that drug use was involved. This evening he and his friends had gone on a spray-painting rampage targeting five of the churches in our small Northern California coastal town. It is too long a story to recount here, but our family began a descent into hell that lasted for the next sixth months. Our days and nights were filled with police visits, arrests, hatred, probation officers, drug tests, arguments, counseling, injuries, surgery, marital strain, broken relationships with our other children, loneliness, threats, suicide attempts, mental health interventions, wondering where God had gone, Peter's incarceration and placement into *Teen Challenge Boys' Ranch*, and a move to Arkansas . . . like I said, hell on earth (not a reference to Arkansas). In April 2013, after a couple of months in the wonderful residential treatment program of the TC Boys' Ranch, Peter gave his broken life and heart to Jesus and experienced transformation. We all began to slowly heal. I hadn't written a word since the night our ordeal began, and it was awhile before I could bring myself to even post to the long abandoned Facebook group. So I posted:

June 27, 2013

Wow! You set out to write a light-hearted book about how the Devil has been trying to kill you since childhood, and he goes turbo with multiple attempts since the beginning of November 2012—just days after I started posting to this group. I have been hit with severe injury, death threats, surgery, kidney stone attacks, severe illness, and yesterday . . . a brown recluse spider bite for which treatment included blood tests, two hip injections, salves, ice, and, I'm not kidding ... being zapped with a Taser multiple times around the wound site (which apparently stops the venom from spreading the necrosis).

Well, to Hell with him! (And I mean that literally.) I am going to start posting new stories today!

And I did. Though not on the planned daily basis. Heavy travel and a bout with malaria further delayed me (replacing *M is for Moose* with *M is for Mosquito*). I finally posted the final chapter, *Z is for Zealots,* on the 26th of July. I can't tell you how happy and relieved this made both Louise and me. While I undoubtedly still have a target painted on me by Satan, I can at least concentrate on ducking his salvos with this book in the can.

May these stories cause you to glorify God and trust Him more!

Brian Hogan
University of the Nations, Kailua–Kona, Hawaii
Friday, August 15, 2014

Acknowledgments

God the Father, for adopting me as His son and never once regretting it despite countless provocations.

Supporters and co-laborers: Kevin and Laura Sutter, Scotty Meades, Youth With A Mission's International Frontier Mission Leadership Team, Dag Jakobsen, Andrew and Kristin Friedman, Barbara Friedman, Dale and Dorothy Jensen, Los Osos Christian Fellowship, Randy and Anne Nash, New Heights of Fayetteville, Harvest Christian Center of El Paso, Patrick and Maria O'Cock, James and Krissie Dunn, Don and Darleen Trousdale, Jon and Kaylynn Jordan, Magnolia Park UMC of Burbank, June Glennon, Jerry and Sally Salino, Michael and Sondra Miller, Mary Manes, Donn and Diane McClish, Brian and Eileen Rowe, Leslie and Scott Lemmon, Scott and Anne Lovell, Matt and Holly Baker, Ray and Judy Ruddell, Elizabeth Dolaghan, Eric Anderson, Brian and Debbie Holden, Elaine and Myron Webster, Bev Swanson, Erich and Glady Protz, Mark Gilliland, Richard and Naomi Dassow, Frank and Debbie Buffam, Lori Blakely, Steve and Judy Sharp, and my late mother, Carol Hadford.

The Author's Salon Feedback team: Jocelyn Dost, Elizabeth Mitchell, Leslie Lemmon, Tisha Catena, Jennifer Rose-Soule, LaurieAnn Powell, Evelyn Stillwell, Melinda Johnson, Sue Story, Donna Christian, Rich Solis, Janette Cokeley, Derek Anderson, Christy Graham, and Louise Hogan.

Production team: Elizabeth Mitchell for a heroic job of editing. There is nothing greater than the heart of a volunteer. My favorite Dave— Dave Hudson for his wonderful cover art.

Foreword

If ever a man of this modern age was destined to epitomize John Newton of old, that man is my friend Brian Hogan.

As Newton hymned:

> *"Through many dangers, toils and snares*
> *I have already come."*

So too does Brian Hogan's startling *warts and all* life story reveal—after multiple encounters with bullies at school, a childhood escape from a pedophile, danger from impassioned Muslims in Egypt, appendicitis linked with a staph infection on the edge of Asia's Gobi desert, near-death from malaria in Mozambique and fugu poisoning in Thailand, not to mention entrapment by corrupt officials in Tanzania and a scurrilous cab driver in Bethlehem—that our Brian is still pressing ahead in his service for God.

And now for a little secret: all of the above daunting challenges are just part of the many crises he has faced!

Yet Hogan's gauntlet of hazards just as truly also affirms the next line of John Newton's famously autobiographical hymn:

> *"'Tis grace hath brought me safe thus far*
> *and grace will lead me home."*

Indeed, both men travelled the world, Newton as a slave trader who became a man of faith and an advocate for emancipation, Hogan as a teenage miscreant who—captured by the love of Christ—inspired a handful of Christians in Mongolia to multiply their numbers phenomenally and then proceeded to teach bands of believers in dozens of other nations to "go thou and do likewise." Across America and around the world, Brian Hogan has become an example of what it *takes* to manifest Christ in ways that offer to "some from every tribe, language, people and nation" emancipation from the power of evil.

Reader, to prepare yourself for what awaits you here, I recommend that you first draw several deep breaths and then, as you begin reading, pray that you will still have some adrenalin left in your glands by the time you get to the last page. It will take an extra ounce or two to thank God adequately for the impact of the Hogan saga.

Don Richardson

Missionary Statesman and Author
of *Heaven Wins, Peace Child,*
Lords of the Earth & *Eternity in Their Hearts*

Grandson: *A book?*

Grandpa: *That's right. When I was your age, television was called books. And this is a special book. It was the book my father used to read to me when I was sick, and I used to read it to your father. And today I'm gonna read it to you.*

Grandson: *Has it got any sports in it?*

Grandpa: *Are you kidding? Fencing, fighting, torture, revenge, giants, monsters, chases, escapes, true love, miracles...*

Grandson: *Doesn't sound too bad. I'll try to stay awake.*

Grandpa: *Oh, well, thank you very much, very nice of you. Your vote of confidence is overwhelming.*

—The Princess Bride

A is for Abyss

(Summer 1975)

They had as king over them the angel of the Abyss...

—Revelation 9:11 (NIV)

C alico Ghost Town, located in the Calico Mountains of the Mojave Desert near Yermo, California, was the stage on which my stepbrothers, cousins, and I played out our fantasies of a wild boomtown life in the lawless old west. My mother and I, and later our blended family, would camp here and meet my grandparents, aunt, uncle and cousins from Las Vegas; Calico provided a good halfway point between Glendale and *Glitter Gulch*. As soon as our Ford Grand Torino station wagon pulled into a campsite, my step-brothers and I would spill out of the *way-back* in a flutter of comic books and snack packaging and tear off to explore the painted hills in a hunt for adventure. My parents complained bitterly about this behavior as they had the quaint and romantic notion of a campsite carefully pitched and laid out in a burst of loving family cooperation and togetherness. The fact this never happened, even once, did not completely disabuse them of this notion. Looking back, I feel a wave of sentimental awe at those two deluded and brave people and their unflagging and hopeful quixotic faith that we would come around.

I had three stepbrothers: Scott, Eric, and Derek. The two with the rhyming names were redheaded twins and a year younger than me. They often spoke in a private language meant to sound like the squeaking of mice. Imagine the verbal equivalent of fingernails on a chalkboard and you'll have it. Eric was fairly transparent and alternatively friendly or angry, and Derek was *the good child*—careful in what he projected to adults—and sneaky. Apart from these quirks, Erik and Derek were both fun and uncomplicated, so they were my preferred companions. The Calico trip recounted here came two and a half years after my mom, Carol, married Dave Anderson, the father of three boys. I had gone from being an only child of a single parent with four doting grandparents to being the eldest (by a mere 4 months!) of four boys in a raucous family of six. *The Brady Bunch* we were not! Scott was the same age as I (13 on this trip) and a whole lot stronger. Built like a tank, Scott knew how to intimidate the rest of us with violence and his short fuse. My new stepfather used his hand and belt on all of us, but from the beginning, I took the brunt of Dave's disciplinary outbursts. Having an adult strike me was a new and disturbing phenomenon. My mom taught me to use my words and never my fists, but my words infuriated Dave to the point of inarticulate rage. My stepbrothers had grown up with physicality and knew how to avoid a lot of it. To say I was in an adjustment free-fall is putting it mildly.

Anyway, this one bright, hot and glaring Mojave afternoon, the four of us headed up into the closest hills. The hills surrounding the played-out former silver boom town

of Calico are still as colorful and *purty as a gal's calico skirt.* These multi-colored hills fascinated us because they were littered with rusty treasures (maybe we'll find a gun or some dynamite!) and honeycombed with shafts

Beautiful but dangerous "mine field"

where miners had pickaxed and blasted their way into the rock looking for the ever elusive mother lode. After some poking around and slipping and sliding down a tailings heap, we decided to play hide-and-seek. We did "1 — 2 —

3 NOT IT!" and Scott lost. He didn't explode and just started immediately counting to 100, so I got the twins to run with me over to a mine entrance hidden down in a gully between two hills. I was sure Scott hadn't seen it earlier when we'd been exploring. Just a dozen feet past the wood beam framed entrance, the light seemed to fail completely, and the tunnel stretched out ahead into inky darkness—a stark change from the blinding desert sun.

I led the way, walking ever more slowly as we entered the pitch dark with rough rock walls pressing in on us. Those walls and the rubble-strewn floor quickly became my only points of contact with anything outside my own mind. It was surreal how absolute the darkness was, and we quickly forgot the danger of betraying our hiding places with noise as we chattered about not being able to see our fingers fluttering directly in front of our eyes, much less each other. I continued to urge my only slightly less foolhardy twin brothers deeper into the cave-like, horizontal shaft. It was perfect! In the inky and utter blackness, Scott would literally have to touch us to find us!

About a minute of slowly shuffling further back into the bowels of the earth, my skin began to crawl. I started imagining nameless cave dwelling creatures standing right in front of me waiting for my face to bump into their matted and hairy chests. I whispered to the twins, who each had a hand on my shoulder, "Stop. I am getting down on my hands and knees. We don't know what's ahead." I went to the cavern floor and began to inch forward, Eric and Derek alongside and only slightly behind me.

A moment later, I almost lost control of bodily functions. My hand went into an abyss. The floor had disappeared in front of us. I stopped dead at the edge and tried to regain control of my breathing. The twins stopped as well. When a morsel of my courage returned, I felt about and discovered there was no longer any bottom to our cavern from wall to wall and as far forward as I dared to lean and reach. There was a vertical shaft directly in front of us, and we had come within inches of plumbing its depths. Whatever had given me the overwhelming impulse to stop and drop had, without a doubt, saved our very young and foolish skins. We backed slowly away from the precipice, got to our feet, and began feeling our way back out along the wall. Once out in the sun again, Scott quickly spotted us and beat us back to the goal, winning the round. The sensation of still sucking oxygen trumped the sting of losing the game.

B

B is for Bear

(Winter 1978)

"The best way of being kind to bears is not to be very close to them."
— Margaret Atwood, *MaddAddam*

Every year I was at Crescenta Valley High School, the Science Department organized a week-long learning experience in Yosemite National Park. The Yosemite Institute led groups of teens from all over in a hands-on experience with ecology and creativity. I loved it! Our trip was always in January, which meant waterfalls frozen into fantastical pillars of glistening ice with huge spray cones at the base resembling snow pyramids, and huge ice chunks floating down the Merced River. During the half of the week spent in the backcountry above the valley, cross-country skiing and snowshoeing were a thrilling part of the venue. Yosemite, at most times our nation's busiest and most congested park, puts on her most gorgeous gowns in winter—with almost no one around to marvel. I'd gone my freshman year, and Yosemite hooked me like a drug. I couldn't decide which I loved more—the intense focus on my favorite thing—nature, or the way my peers interacted as soon as we left behind the cliques and politics of our campus in the L.A. smog. Real friendships developed with kids who wouldn't have spared a glance for me back at school. The Institute staff was great at making my quirky enthusiasm seem like an asset, not only to me, but to my classmates as well. It was a yearly week of bliss in what was mostly a long tough miserable slog for me.

My junior year I was one of the first signed up for the trip and fairly thrummed with anticipation as the date approached. The previous year's trip had been a rocky one for me. I had run afoul of both the chaperones and Yosemite Park Curry Company when a battle between cabins had resulted in a broken window. This had not been the only incident and I was not the only perpetrator, but I was the one left holding the bag (and the bill for a new window). There had been talk of banning me from future trips, but Ron Abarta, the science teacher, was a believer in Jesus and second chances for the repentant. And I was very repentant when I figured out the consequences. So, I was on my best behavior.

It was our first evening in Yosemite Valley. The view that greeted us when our bus cleared the tunnel was like what I imagined for Narnia in winter: sheer granite cliffs with snow dusting every protrusion towering over a valley floor resembling a cake with thick white frosting softened by dark pines. It actually did seem to take your breath away for a moment. After checking in to our WOBs—cabins *WithOut Bath*—we bolted down our dinners at the dining hall, and with Mr. and Mrs. Abarta's blessing, headed over to the ice skating rink about a mile from our cabins. Soon we were all skated up and out on the ice, gliding in circles and inventing endless games to keep it interesting.

Someone streaked by and grabbed my cap from my head. Realizing it was a local kid starting a new game, I tore off in hot pursuit. Soon we were all in ad-hoc teams playing *steal the hat* and having an absolute ball. After a couple hours in the cold thin air, these exertions winded me pretty good. I skated to the side and collapsed on a bench to catch my breath as the games went on. I soon noticed my feet throbbing inside the rental skates. I wear size thirteen and never seemed to end up with skates that fit me. Unlacing, I pulled my sore foot out for a breather. The sight of blood on my sock surprised me. I had literally been playing and laughing too hard to notice as my feet first blistered and then tore open by the ill-fitting ice skates. Reluctantly, I determined I was done for the night and needed to get my regular shoes back on and limp back to my WOB. I told my cabin mate I was walking back and left the rink.

It didn't take very long at all to walk far enough that the bright lights of the rink failed, and I was in the dark. I wished I'd brought a flashlight, but thinking ahead in terms of flashlight, umbrella, or payphone money was not my long suit in those heady teen years. The main road was straight as it traversed the length of the valley, and without any turns to navigate, I really didn't feel any trepidation about a walk in the dark. Back home in Glendale, our neighborhood was nestled into the Verdugo Mountains, and I was used to sneaking out at midnight for hikes to the radio towers at the top. So other than being far chillier, everything felt normal on this walk in the dark.

It was a bit unnerving how seldom a car would pass me providing a brilliant moment of illuminated surroundings and a sense of human connectedness before plunging me back into solitude and darkness. Beyond the occasional passing vehicles, Yosemite seemed almost completely deserted and silent. Just as I was really embracing the enveloping sense of utter peace and quiet, I saw another car, only the third, headed in my direction. Feeling proud of having a cautious idea not suggested by Mom, I carefully took three steps sideways off the roadway lest a car sideswipe me in the dark. I felt like a modern version of my 6th great grandfather, Daniel Boone the Pathfinder, for remembering to memorize which shoulder was facing the road and how many steps back I needed to take to be on it. In another couple of seconds, the speeding vehicle was upon me and I could, for a brief moment, see my nearby environs as clear as day.

Directly in front of me and less than six feet away, was a huge black bear! I could see it looking right at me and suddenly, like flipping off a light switch, the car passed, and I was again blind. I froze in midstride like a Greek kouros statue (though a kouros wrapped in knit hat, long underwear, Levi's and a down jacket, rather than nude as is traditional for kouroi). I wondered if I could follow the only advice that I remembered from Boy Scouts and *play dead*. Would the bear think I was dead if I was still standing? Wouldn't collapsing to the ground betray my position while considerably improving the possibility of my demise? Who says bears don't eat freshly dead people? They eat garbage!

It is amazing how many fully formed and very articulate thoughts can race through my mind when I am anticipating the crunch of huge fangs on my pelvic bone. I even tried to remember all I knew about the indigenous bruins. *"The (North) American black bear (Ursus americanus) is a medium-sized bear native to North America. It is the continent's smallest and most common bear species."* It is small comfort to realize one could have blundered into a larger bear species in the pitch-dark night, or that black bear encounters probably happen to everyone since they are "the most common bear species." At this moment I would have had more options open to me if I had known less—in other words, if I were limited to the knowledge of the nursery where bears are cuddly and named things like Pooh and Paddington. I was determined not to even breathe. I remembered a ranger telling me, "The animal (we were discussing rattlesnakes) is more frightened than you are." How do they determine that? Maybe the bear was going to play dead. It was certainly a more adaptive survival strategy for her (or him) as there was no way I would stop to munch on a dead bear next to the road. I strained to hear any sound of impending furry doom, and absolute snow-muffled silence greeted my ears. It seemed to be a complete standoff.

It wasn't very long (not long enough) before the need to breath began to war against the far more sensible plan to silently hide from the bear. I eventually had to attempt a noiseless gasp for air (try that!). My greatest desire was for this bear to keep on believing I was no longer in the land of the living. How comprehensive is the medical knowledge of a bear anyway? Surely breathing isn't a deal killer for calling a D.O.A. Right? Oh God, please help me, I prayed silently. When I prayed, which was seldom during my teen years, I was, in general, a fan of the silent prayer—and in this moment as I prayed, gratitude that God was a mind reader filled my spirit to overflow levels.

After what seemed an eternity and was probably a minute or two, I began to think that if the bear was at all afraid and tried to sneak off or run away, he had a pretty good chance of running directly into me. I mean, I knew which way I was facing, but the bear was not descended from Boone and could be experiencing some bewilderment. As soon as I had prayed for help, the idea of making noise—on purpose!—came to me. If I clapped and sang "la-la-la" loudly, the bear would be able to head the opposite direction, if he so desired. The horror of a scared and shocked animal slamming right into me in his escape and the two of us going down in a flailing rolling heap became untenable. With my heart in my throat, I began to make a racket. I clapped loudly and rapidly, stomped my feet,

yelled and sang. My hope was that I sounded huge and terrifying. Of course, with all the noise I was making, I
wouldn't have heard the bear in front of me or Disney-
land's whole dang *Country Bear Jamboree* moving away. Realizing this flaw in the plan, I decided to keep up my one-
man-band and put it into forward gear. I began to walk
with stomping steps while hollering and clapping, trying
with all my might to imagine a bear scampering off in the
opposite direction with his stubby tail between his legs. I
kept that up for at least 25 yards down the road and then
continued swiftly along to my cabin.

I wish I had a more satisfying ending, but I never laid eyes
on that bear again after the car lights went out for us. I just
knew I'd come far closer to a possibly fatal mauling than I
ever wanted to be.

C

C is for Cliff

(Spring 1988)

Serving as Dorm Parents for a dozen Navajo boys aged six through twelve was Louise and my first experience in cross-cultural ministry. Navajo Christian Academy was an outreach of Navajo Gospel Mission located on a compound at Hardrock, the geographical center of the Navajo Indian Reservation.

During our limited free time, when the boys were in school or home on weekends, we enjoyed visiting their families in their encampments and exploring the high desert badlands that surrounded us. I've always had a thing for abandoned buildings and historic sites. Out on the reservation we had to be pretty careful about entering an abandoned home because the Navajos have a strong death taboo. If someone dies in a home the family must abandon that *hogan* (Navajo house). Furthermore, everyone would avoid entering that hogan except for witches—a group known to violate cultural taboos. For similar reasons Navajos also avoided Anasazi (ancient 13th-century cliff dwellers) archaeological sites with the unassailable logic that everyone who used to live there was now dead.

A coworker had introduced me to a site called Pottery Hill that was relatively close to our mission station. In the middle of nowhere, and only reachable by dirt track, Pottery Hill stood alone in the desert. Ancient pottery shards littered the slopes of this mini mesa. Every piece was like an antique work of art with designs pressed into the clay and painted patterns. It was in such an isolated location, observation by locals was a real unlikelihood.

So when my aunt and young cousins came out for a visit from Maryland, Pottery Hill was one of many sites I planned to share with them. My Aunt Barbara was my mom's youngest sister and had always seemed to me to totter somewhere between the parent and child status as I grew. She was my *fun* aunt. Her two sons were my favorite little cousins. Danny (14) and Andy (10) both tended to hero-worship "Cousin Brian" which further endeared them to me. On a bright sunny day, four of us crowded into my pickup truck with its camper shell, and soon we were bumping across the desert toward Pottery Hill. I parked the truck at the base of the hill and clambered out along with my Aunt Barbara and my cousins. As we made our way slowly up the steep hill, we immediately began to find beautiful examples of ancient pottery—all broken in pieces. My personal theory was the ancients used this mesa as a place of sacrifice and actually smashed their bowls on-site. Upon reaching the top we had fun showing each other what we'd found and discovering new pieces everywhere we looked. Danny and I came across a fairly large hole dug right into the top of the hill. I saw something curious sticking out of the wall of the hole and hopped down inside to get a better look. What I saw sticking out of the dirt looked like the spout of an ancient Anasazi teapot. Without stopping to examine the absurdity of ancient Anasazi drinking tea, I began to loosen the dirt holding the protrusion in place with my finger. To my disappointment, it came loose much quicker than an entire teapot would have, and I found myself holding about half of a hollow human bone. I was standing in a looted grave.

I immediately dropped the bone and clambered out of the grave. The thought any of my Navajo friends might discover what I had just done horrified me. They would've had to break off contact with me. Taking a deep breath, I walked over to the edge of the sandstone tabletop we were standing on. Looking out over the beautiful painted desert, I attempted to collect my racing thoughts. Suddenly and without warning, the ledge I was standing on broke loose on the top of the mesa. As I began to plummet straight down, I spun around and tried to grab the top of the cliff. My reward for this was the rock surface caught me under the chin as I sped by—shattering my jaw. Before I could form another thought, I had fallen 40 feet. I hit the boulder-strewn slope and slid downhill for 15 or 20 feet before coming to a stop, broken and bleeding.

I was still conscious and somehow managed to get to my feet and begin to stagger toward my red Toyota truck. I knew I needed help, and it was a long drive away. Aunt Barbara had been taking a photo of me when the cliff gave way and watched me drop out of her viewfinder. She and my cousins caught up with me while I was still 10 yards away from the truck. From their horrified looks, I got the impression I looked at least as bad as I felt. Seeping and bleeding abrasions covered much of my body; my hands and knees were in particularly bad shape. Blood was running out of my mouth and I was spitting shards of broken teeth. My aunt helped me into the passenger seat in the cab of the truck while the boys scrambled into the back. The problem was my aunt had no idea where we were in relation to the road or to the nearest medical facilities. Aunt Barbara was thankful she'd learned to drive a stick shift so that she could handle my truck. We started driving slowly across the desert. And although I had to pause and spit a mouthful of blood out the window about every 30 seconds, I was able, by drawing arrows on the windshield, to get us back onto the dirt road after about 10 minutes. At this point, my aunt asked me which way the hospital was. The closest help was now Keam's Canyon Hospital, a forty-five minute drive across the Hopi mesas. I tried to say, "Keam's Canyon" to my aunt, but it turns out this is an incredibly hard thing to say with a broken jaw. It came out something like, "eeee awh awh". Repeating it didn't seem to help, so I dipped my finger into the blood pooling in my mouth and wrote "Keam's Canyon" on the windshield in front of me. I also knew of a little trailer that served as a clinic in Kykotsmovi, Arizona, on our route and about 14 miles ahead. I indicated the direction to drive, and we took off as fast and as safely possible down the rutted dirt road.

Struggling against the effects of shock, I managed to direct us to the clinic trailer. As we pulled up, we could see the *Closed* sign from the truck. Aunt Barbara went into the clinic to get help, but the staff refused to give any treatment to a non-Native-American. They called the Keam's Canyon hospital, and an ambulance was dispatched. We were obliged to wait for its arrival. I was then transferred into the ambulance, and we sped off east with my aunt, cousins and truck following in our wake. This was good for me because I was having trouble staying conscious, and giving directions was proving difficult.

Next I knew several people were helping me out of the ambulance and into the emergency room. A doctor examined me after a short wait. He guessed I had broken my jaw, and none of the other injuries seemed very serious. He also informed us I was the wrong color to receive care from Indian Health Services. The long and short of it is IHS doctors are very reluctant to serve non-Indians because white people sue for malpractice and Indians don't. He was willing only to give me a shot of Demerol for the pain, some gauze to hold against my mouth, a hospital blanket to cushion me a bit, and his recommendation that we drive quickly to the hospital in Flagstaff, Arizona. This was especially disheartening because our detour to Keam's Canyon had taken us about an hour out of our way to Flagstaff. We now had a two hour 35 minute drive. At least Louise knew what was happening as my aunt had called her while we were waiting for the doctor. We couldn't bump back down the dirt roads to pick up Louise in Hardrock, so my aunt and cousins needed to continue ambulance duties. This time a bed of sorts was made for me in the back of the pickup, and my cousin Danny stayed back to watch over me while his brother rode shotgun up front. Even with the smoother paved roads, with each bump the pain of the bones grinding together was intense. Even so I did manage to fall asleep several times during the long journey.

I awoke to yet another scene of medical professionals helping me out of the truck and into an emergency room. X-rays were taken, and it was determined I needed surgery to repair my jaw. I'd also lost my wisdom tooth on the bottom right side, and the corresponding tooth on the top no longer had a strike plate and required extraction. That evening a fellow missionary brought Louise and our daughter Melody down to Flagstaff, and after visiting me in my hospital room, they checked into a hotel. My aunt and cousins were flying back to Maryland a day or so later anyway, so their trip was almost over. The oral surgeon we'd chosen was sick, so I ended up spending almost a week in the hospital before surgery. Hideously swollen, my head resembled a melon. I had trouble talking and wrote a lot of notes to communicate. I was intentionally vague about where the accident had happened, not wanting to alienate my Navajo friends. They see a direct correlation between being in a grave and handling of bone and then almost immediately falling off the cliff. I didn't share their worldview, but I was sure foul spirits were involved in this accident.

Eventually the surgeon showed up, performed the operation successfully, and I wound up with a steel plate in my jaw. In follow-up visits, I learned to my amusement, I was his only patient with a broken jaw who had not incurred the injury in a bar fight. Upon my release from the hospital I was able to resume my duties as Dorm Dad. The major problem was, with my jaw wired shut, I was unable to get the boys' attention when they were misbehaving. Try yelling with your teeth clenched. I also needed to recruit a stamp licker when mailing out our newsletter, and the liquid diet began to drive me just a little crazy after a while. I had Louise put enchiladas and pizza slices in the blender just to get some variety. It seemed like forever, but eventually my reconstructed jaw healed enough to be unwired and life returned to normal.

D

D is for Demons

(1969 & 1970)

Submit yourselves, then, to God. Resist the devil, and he will flee from you.

—James 4:7 (NIV)

Growing up, I spent a lot of time with my grandparents. My father was long gone and my mom worked full-time at Children's Hospital of Los Angeles as a pediatric nurse, so we needed both sets of grandparents to keep me under supervision. They loved it. God had compensated me for our broken home with four grandparents who loved me to death. My father's parents, Nana and Papa Hogan, lived just across town, and I spent frequent weekends at their house. My mom's parents, Nana Alice and Papa Jim, lived halfway across the country, in Blue Island, Illinois. They weren't close enough for short visits, so I stayed with them every summer. The summer I was seven, Papa Jim took me to see downtown Chicago at night. Chicago was his city, and he was a fountain of historical knowledge. I remember riding around and having buildings and street corners pointed out to me along with stories of personal and historic significance. Papa Jim was a Chicago cabbie during the late 1920s and had incredible tales to share about Al Capone and other colorful Prohibition Era figures.

We ended this particular evening at Buckingham Fountain. Chicago lights up this landmark spectacularly

Buckingham Fountain postcard with those trees in the background

every night, and my grandpa thought it a perfect finale to our night out. However, hyperactive seven-year-olds lack an attention span for lighted fountain displays. Before long, I managed to wander off down one of the long tree-lined avenues that led away from the fountain. Soon I was alone beneath the lines of tall dark trees; their branches blocking out even the moon and stars.

Feeling swallowed by the darkness surrounding me, I realized I was completely alone and all at once a thought slipped in: "There are witches in the trees." Instantly I felt more terror than I dreamed possible clutch at my heart. I spun around to run back to the light. I could sense malevolent presences above dropping toward me. Intense fear overwhelmed and paralyzed me. I felt my knees buckle, and I curled into a self-protective fetal position. Barely breathing, I felt I had only seconds to live. Whatever they were . . . they were closing in. I screwed my eyes as tightly shut as I could and waited for the claws I was sure were about to pierce my back. I remember my mind screaming out, "Jesus, save me!"

"What's wrong, son? Can I help you?" asked a deep and kindly voice. Still so terrified I was almost wetting myself, I was afraid to look up. I felt gentle hands laid on my shoulder and my side, so I pried open my eyes. I was both completely stunned and relieved by what I saw. To my seven-year-old mind, I doubt that anything could have so convinced me God himself had shown up to help me. A priest standing over me in his long black robe and shining white collar looking concerned and kind at the same time. I began to babble, warning him all about the witches. I'm sure I didn't make any sense, but he gathered me up, hugged me and spoke calming words, and led me by the hand back to my grandfather. Papa Jim had noticed by this point I was missing, and he was walking through the crowd looking for me. He wrapped me in a big hug and thanked the priest for bringing me back. I held on to my grandpa and wouldn't let go. I couldn't seem to get anyone to really understand what happened to me, nor was I was able to explain it convincingly. But I knew God had saved me because I'd called out to Him. Little kids have the disadvantage of almost no knowledge and experience, but the advantage of not questioning things they sense spiritually. As I grew and learned, I came to the conclusion the witches had actually been demons—dark spirits with an assignment against me. Regardless of definition, it was still too real, even years later, to explain away.

It wasn't as though this was an isolated incident. Less than a year later foul spirits attacked me again. This time much closer to home—on Hollywood Boulevard with my Papa Hogan. Now, while Nana and Papa Anderson were, in equal measures loving and strict with me, my other grandparents were just as loving, but far more lenient. Where one set felt I needed to hear the word "no" quite a bit, the other two only seemed to have a single answer for all my requests: yes. I had taken advantage of this while visiting Hollywood and asked my grandpa to take me to the Hollywood Wax Museum. I loved history and was intrigued for that reason, but I also longed to be scared and knew from school friends they had a cool Chamber of Horrors.

For some reason, at this point in my life I had a fascination with dead people. I would watch television shows with my Nana Hogan, and whenever someone got shot I'd ask "Is he dead, Nana?" She would answer in the affirmative, and I would shoot back: "Then where's the blood?"

So, as my grandpa and I walked through the wax museum, while I enjoyed scenes from *Gone with the Wind, Hello Dolly!*, and the grinning effigy of Marilyn Monroe[1], I was looking forward to the room where they kept the dead people and blood. When we finally entered the famed Chamber of Horrors, my heart was racing. The actuality was a bit of a letdown. A number of the exhibits were movie monsters: Dracula, Frankenstein, Mr. Hyde and the Wolfman. These were not what I was looking for. I didn't find them frightening. I'd been to Universal Studios several times (it was only 3 miles from my house) and had seen behind the scenes on these guys. However, further along the darkened corridor of chills was a bloody tableau of the famous St. Valentine's Day Massacre from Chicago history. My other grandfather had actually pointed out to me the building where this took place and told me he'd had his shoes repaired there just two days before the shootings. So, not only did I have a personal connection to this crime, but there were bodies and blood galore—all depicted in vibrant wax! It was the perfect storm for a morbid eight-year-old.

The thought of explaining to my mother why I was screaming with nightmares every night was making Papa Hogan queasy. He knew well she would not approve of this choice of diversions. He ended up hurrying me

---

[1] Neither Papa Hogan nor I had any idea that Norma Jean "Marilyn Monroe" Baker, was also a Hogan and our relative. Marilyn was my 6th cousin, and Papa's 5th cousin—with one removal from both.

through the rest of the Chamber of Horrors and back out into lighter fare. A few minutes later, I managed to slip away on my own. I just had to have another look at all those dead mobsters. I circled back into the darkened Chamber of Horrors and stared at the St. Valentine's Day Massacre exhibit. I began to feel an almost electric prickle of fear move across my body and discovered to my dismay I was completely alone. Suddenly I had a repeat of my Buckingham Fountain discernment: something evil was there to destroy me. I was too overwhelmed to move, call out, or run. Again I dropped to the floor and curled into a tight fetal position—my arms around my ears and hands clasped behind my head. I felt malevolent entities all around me closing in. In my mind I called out, "Jesus help me!"

Seconds later I heard a female voice asking, "What's wrong?" I looked up to find three nuns in full habit surrounding me. Flooded with relief, I let them help me to my feet and take me to my grandpa. The whole incident had happened so quickly, he hadn't time to become concerned. I didn't even try to describe to Papa Hogan what had happened. He wasn't the sort of grandpa you talked to about spiritual things. I knew I'd been targeted by numerous, hateful and completely evil entities, and God had rescued me. It was a nice twist to send nuns this time to save the little Methodist boy. I am convinced I needed the uniforms to know the cavalry had indeed arrived. For whatever reason, it had happened twice, and I had no idea why.

E

E is for Exhaustion

(1984)

It was the Friday before Labor Day, and Louise and I had been married just two and a half months. We decided to take advantage of the holiday weekend and go south to La Crescenta, California to visit my mom and new stepdad. After working eight-hour shifts, Louise in an electronic assembly plant and me painting the museum at Morro Bay State Park for the California Conservation Corp, we hopped into our blue Datsun B-210 for the four-hour drive south. I took first shift driving down US 101 and, north of Santa Barbara, decided to take a shortcut past Lake Cachuma on Highway 154. We had a Christian rock cassette playing loudly in an attempt to stave off drowsiness. Both of us were really feeling the effects of a full day's work and the long drive in the hot California summer sun. Opposing traffic was really quite heavy as the masses were fleeing Los Angeles for the holiday weekend. Heading south meant our lane was almost empty. We felt lucky to escape the heavy northbound traffic just across the centerline. We passed the tiny Danish town of Solvang and were driving alongside and above the lake. Louise was asleep, and my eyelids were so heavy . . . .

Suddenly the whole world seemed to be crashing, spinning, bouncing, and bumping. There was a final jolt and tremendous noise followed by a cloud of choking dust. Everything was still except for the cassette deck which continued to blare Randy Stonehill singing, "I've got news for you. This is not a game. I've got news for you. Are you listening?" As the dust cleared we were staring through the broken front windshield at a giant boulder, but something else was wrong. Everything was upside down. After determining neither of us was hurt, we both released our seat belts. Big mistake! Our car may have been permanently out of commission, but the law of gravity was still working just fine. We both plunged down to the ceiling onto a carpet of shards of shattered glass. Each of us received numerous fine cuts that bled profusely. Somehow we managed to open the doors and crawl from the wreckage. Finding ourselves at the bottom of a hill next to the crushed upside-down husk of our blue Datsun was wrenchingly disorienting. We scrambled uphill to the side of the highway. A number of cars had stopped and the people were running over to where we had gone over the side. They seemed very surprised to see us and were very concerned about our appearance. Even though I protested I felt fine, they were afraid I had a horrible head injury and insisted I lie still on my back. It was the blood from the small cuts that had them so worried. Both of us were fine, but the car was a total loss.

Our Datsun was now upside down, facing north, and suspended neatly between two huge boulders. Somehow while sleeping, we had managed to cross a solid line of northbound traffic, plunge over the side of the highway, flip completely over end-to-end, and land with the trunk resting on one boulder and the hood on another. The only part of the vehicle uncrushed was the compartment where we'd been sitting. Louise and I ended up waiting for the tow truck, and then hitching a ride with the driver back into Solvang where we stayed with one of Louise's college swimming teammates. My mother and step-dad drove up the next morning and brought us back to La Crescenta. But before leaving Solvang, we went by the junkyard and retrieved our Randy Stonehill tape from the wreckage.

The view from where we went off the highway.

F

F is for Fugu
(Spring 2008)

Youth With A Mission's International Frontier Mission Leadership Team (IFMLT) moves their yearly gathering around the globe, and in the Spring of 2008, Thailand was our venue. Louise has missed many opportunities over the years to interact with our coworkers due to responsibilities at home, so we were excited God worked out provision and timing for this rare opportunity to travel as a couple to Chaing Rai. After the IFMLT meetings concluded, we booked a week at a backpackers' resort run by the Akha hill tribe. We hoped for some much needed *us time*.

Our time in the hill country was everything we'd hoped. Days spent hiking to waterfalls, swimming in jungle pools, soaking in hot springs, making new friends, sharing stories with them, and experiencing the exotic culture of our wonderful and loving Akha hosts were God's prescriptions for our rejuvenation. All too soon our time came to an end, and we had to fly back to Bangkok for an overnight layover on our return to California. Bangkok was hot, sweaty, and chaotically busy compared to our quiet mountain retreat. Nevertheless, we were loath to waste our one evening in this mega-city, so we plunged into the rushing river of humanity in a quest for dinner.

As we walked around Bangkok looking for a good sea-food restaurant with reasonable prices, it felt as if we were embracing the ADD I've always struggled with. We were constantly distracted from our search by the lively sights and sounds of Bangkok street life. We stopped for foot massages which were so cheap and luxurious that a half hour later we each indulged in another. A garish sign lured us inside a beauty salon offering ear wax removal. This new experience turned out to be weird, frightening, embarrassing, and very effective. To recover we snacked on little treats we found in stands along the way. The highlight of this treat-finding excursion was attempting to consume a huge diving water beetle, almost two inches long. Its carapace was so tough that repeated bites failed to even dent it. We were near giving up on beetle-eating when an old man took pity on us and demonstrated on a beetle he bought for himself. The trick, it turns out, is to squeeze the beetle so its guts eject from its butt—an appetizing display. Then you happily eat the beetle's now suddenly exterior interior. Yum!

Eventually the lateness of the hour convinced us to take a pedicab and rely on the driver's knowledge and feet to find dinner. He deposited us in front of a lavishly decorated seafood restaurant with no other businesses in the vicinity. As soon as we paid him, our driver sped off, leaving us with little choice—go in or go hungry! We opted for *in* and were relieved to see the many patrons, cleanliness, upscale atmosphere, and almost-reasonable prices. Louise ordered a large broiled sea bass, while I went for the lobster. Both were delicious, and we felt overall the evening had turned out quite a success.

Leaving the restaurant, we could not find any taxis in the immediate vicinity. Walking to a busier street seemed our only option. After a couple of blocks on foot, I noticed a buzzing sensation in my fingertips and lips. I mentioned this to Louise, but neither of us thought much of it at the time. I became more concerned when I realized I'd lost all feeling in my fingertips, lips, and nose, less than 20 minutes after leaving the restaurant. When I told Louise, she remarked it was certainly weird but would probably go away by morning. I figured that was true and tried rather unsuccessfully to ignore the annoying lack of feeling. I kept nervously tapping these extremities every few minutes to check if they were still sensationless. Upon returning to our hotel room, I found my toes similarly affected. Reminding myself worry never changed anything, I decided a good night's sleep was all I needed to set things right.

In the morning I awoke to bright sunlight streaming through the window and an unchanged situation in my nerve endings. I updated Louise who, slightly more concerned, assured me it would soon pass. Four hours later we were 30,000 feet above the Pacific Ocean and headed for home.

But things didn't get better. My condition continued unchanged for weeks. It wasn't easy to put my condition out of my mind as a hundred things a day reminded me my fingertips lacked their former ability to feel. I made an appointment to see a doctor at a local community clinic in our town. We didn't have insurance for this, but they charged on a sliding scale. The doctor ran a battery of tests and several days later called to assure me the tests indicated there was nothing wrong with me. He didn't say so, but I got the impression he felt my condition was psychosomatic. To be honest, I was beginning to wonder about this myself.

Two and a half months passed with absolutely no improvement. I still had no feeling in my lips, my nose tip, and any of my fingertips or toes. Not really debilitating, my condition was just constantly annoying. Nevertheless, I had to press on with my busy travel schedule and speaking engagements. On June 12th, I was on a flight from San Francisco to Dallas-Fort Worth on my way to a national gathering for Perspectives on the World Christian Movement. United gave me a complimentary upgrade to first class, and I found myself in conversation with my seatmate, a fellow world traveler.

At some point, I mentioned my nerve death condition and the inability of medical science to figure out what was wrong with me. My companion immediately sat forward, looked at me intently, and asked, "Have you traveled to Bangkok recently?"

Mystified by this random change in conversational direction I replied, "Yes. My wife and I were there a few months ago. Actually that's where this thing first hit me."

"Did you have seafood in a restaurant?"

"Yes, we did. Why do you ask?" In an instant I remembered walking away from that restaurant feeling a buzzing sensation in my extremities. I had no time to mention this to my interrogator before he explained his question.

"I've been reading news reports of a scandal in Bangkok involving restaurants serving illegal seafood. The government has begun a crackdown. You, my friend, are suffering from fugu poisoning!"

He went on to explain there was a demand among a wealthy Asian clientele for the flesh of the puffer fish, or fugu. The organs of this fish contain a powerful neurotoxin, and chefs are required to complete special, rigorous training to be able to safely prepare this delicacy. The problem in Bangkok was unlicensed and untrained chefs were responding to

Fugu, AKA Puffer Fish

the demand and serving fugu off-menu and illegally. Several deaths had occurred among fugu eating patrons, while restaurants poisoned other diners by cross-contamination of their food in these kitchens. He explained I was almost certainly the unwitting victim of such cross-contamination. My lobster was likely prepared with a knife used previously on fugu. The small amount of toxin I consumed had merely killed the nerve endings in my extremities rather than shutting down everything until my lungs stopped working and death ensued.

This guy was far more knowledgeable than my doctor, so I pressed him with questions.

"Is the damage permanent? Is there anything that can be done?"

He explained it would take some time, maybe as much as a year, but my nerves would regrow, and feeling would gradually return. I was glad to hear this, as I'd been giving up hope. I thanked my fellow traveler for sharing his knowledge with me, and I thanked my Father in Heaven for arranging to upgrade and seat me next to the one guy who knew what was going on.

By August I had made a full recovery and my tangle with this deadly denizen of the deep had joined my other near misses as a memory.

G

G is for Gang
(1974-1975)

This question:'How do I deal with a bully without becoming a thug in return?' has been with me ever since I was a child.

—Scilla Elworthy

Deep in enemy territory and alone, my heart stopped as someone suddenly grabbed my arm from behind. I spun around expecting to see five or more of my enemies and only saw Scotty, a nerdy bespectacled boy partial to Dungeons and Dragons and other tabletop war games. I was astounded he was alone. Sure, Scotty was a year my senior, but did he really think I spent much of my life fleeing his gang because I was afraid to fight? I ran because until today they'd always outnumbered me.

Scotty seemed to notice his vulnerability as soon as I did. As I advanced, he backed away, keeping up a steady stream of curses and threats. I could see no basis in fact for his verbal bravado, so to help him see his true predicament, I grabbed the front of his shirt and smashed my fist into his mouth. He immediately stopped bleating and started bleeding. I slugged him several more times to make the lesson stick, but I didn't have it in me to return in kind the punishment he and his cohort had generously given me. I let go, and he ran off in the direction of his gang's headquarters. When he had gotten a safe distance from me he yelled back through his tears, "You're going to pay for this, Hogan!" I sprinted in his direction just long enough to see him turn and run for his life. Then I made haste for home in case he raised the gang for a retaliatory raid.

How had I come to this—swinging between victim and victimizer?

Life had become frightening and violent from almost my first day at Rosemont Junior High. It started out as *scrub* hazing (*scrub* = 7th grader). Apparently I was just different enough to be a thug-magnet, and as the torment died away for most of my classmates, a few of us had caught the attention of the bullies. Maybe it was my mouth or my lack of concern about what others thought of me, but it was soon evident there was *blood in the water.* Beyond the usual junior high tormenting, teasing, and shoving, I was the designated victim for one particularly nasty gang. I knew them as *The Burnie McCullum Gang,* though looking back on it, they must have seen themselves differently. Burnie was actually a classmate of mine and the youngest in the gang. His older brother was probably the gang's leader, and all the gang members were in the eighth or ninth grades. I didn't want to know anything about them; in fact, I spent much of my time at school keeping out of their sight.

During school hours they actually went pretty easy on me. They tended to limit their activities to knocking books from my hands, slamming my locker shut, shoving me from behind, and whispering death threats they promised to make good on after school. I had cause to take these threats seriously. When they did catch me off campus I was always beaten, and the beatings were both savage and vicious. Souvenirs of these encounters went home with me in the form of torn shirts, swollen lips, bleeding nose, or blackened eyes. I was justifiably terrified of these kids.

While sitting in class, I spent an inordinate amount of time devising escape routes and ways to avoid The Burnie McCullum Gang. I was supposed to ride the bus the two miles from Rosemont Junior High School in La Crescenta down the hill to my home in Glendale. I had plenty of tickets for the school bus. The bus driver, Manny, had a working arrangement with my stepfather, Dave, owner of Dave's Pies. In exchange for grocery bags full of bus tickets, Dave gave Manny pies. Riding the bus to school was never a problem. There were adult monitors watching as we disembarked. It was going home that was a daily horror. The McCullum Gang rode my bus on purpose even though it was out of their way. They'd exit the bus at my stop or anywhere else I might attempt an escape. The first time they got off at my stop, they caught up with me on the bridge into my neighborhood, Oakmont Woods, and administered a beating in full view of the bus driver. One of them opened my book bag and emptied my textbooks off the side of the bridge into the slimy runoff stream[2] below. After that day, Manny would let me out of the bus, closing the door to give me a running head start, before releasing my pursuers. However, there were still three horrifying blocks to run between the bus stop and home, and I often came perilously close to capture.

One weekend my friend Robert Chapman and I were exploring the storm drains under the streets of La Crescenta. All of these tunnels emptied out into the concrete wash at the base of our neighborhood. We'd map these dark tunnels, our shoes slapping and splashing in the algae-slick trickle of water running along the bottom, connecting the dots of the pinpoints of light trickling down from manhole covers above. From time to time we would climb ladders to intakes along the gutters of the streets above so we could see where we were. Crawling out of one of these intakes that Saturday, I discovered I was less than a block from Rosemont Junior High. A plan began to form.

That Monday, I sat in my last class watching the clock countdown to the bell that meant release. I had thought ahead and already collected all the books I would need that night from my locker. My plan required that I sprint

---

[2] See photo in *U is for Underground*

across the playing fields and off campus as soon as I could get out of the classroom. I had to completely avoid my locker and the bus loading area. As the big classroom clock clicked over and the bell began to ring, I was out of my seat, out the door, and running down the hall toward the exit. Avoiding detection by the gang, I made it off campus and ran the half block down Rosemont Avenue to the storm drain intake. I quickly slid my book bag down into the darkness. The opening was equipped with a barrier— a piece of re-bar welded across the entrance—but I was just slim enough to slide between the bar and the concrete of the gutter. I made it! Safe under the street I was able to walk, albeit hunched over, through two miles of gently downward sloping concrete conduit to the wash. It was much harder to get lost going downhill. Starting from the bottom, the storm canals branched upward like a tree. However, from the uphill ends they all flowed to the same place, and intersections were easy to navigate, even in the dark. As long as it didn't start raining topside, I was completely safe. After just under an hour, I came out into the blinding sunlight of the concrete jacketed river and could see the bridge into my neighborhood just a short distance upstream. Making sure to carefully spy out the bus stop and bridge, I found no evidence of my enemies. I'd guessed correctly. If I didn't enter the bus, neither would they. Having lost their quarry, they'd given up the day's hunt. I clambered up the inclined concrete slope to a gap in the fence where I could get out onto the bridge and walked happy and carefree the rest of the way home.

Predictably the gang was frustrated and enraged when they realized I was consistently giving them the slip day after day. They tried posting lookouts on the various routes away from school, but this proved ineffective, as the same bell released both hunter and prey. They took to patrolling the streets near my friends' homes and other known haunts. I responded by moving carefully and doing all the reconnaissance I could from hidden positions before crossing any open territory. I managed to go several months without taking a beating or anything worse than threats. One day, as I was leaving a friend's house, I let my guard drop. Scotty, a member of the gang patrolling that neighborhood, spotted me and the one-sided fight that began this story ensued.

The next day the incident was the talk of the school. The story of my payback to Scotty was more accurate in the retelling than I thought possible. Apparently, when he found his gang and told them about what I had done, his friends responded not with howls for my blood, but with mockery and laughter. They let Scotty know attacking me on his own was suicide, and he was lucky I allowed him to escape. After that day, I never received another blow or threat from that gang. Two years later, I took up gaming at a shop called *The War Club*, and Scotty actually became a friend. Burney was around until we both graduated from High School, but we avoided each other by tacit mutual agreement. He later became a police officer in Glendale, and every time I visited my parents I was nervous about him pulling me over. Decades later I read he had died in a police helicopter crash. I was saddened to hear of a life cut short and hoped my old nemesis had found some peace, but I did breathe a bit easier when visiting my old hometown.

Even now, after almost forty years, I still struggle with how I settled this conflict. For over thirty years I have been following a Master who tells me to turn the other cheek. This makes sense to me. I agree with Him. Yet, I can't help but think there are people in this world who never come to the end of cheeks they're willing to bloody. How do you stop a bully? What advice do I give my son or grandson? Does resisting evil sometimes mean hitting back? I want to believe even boys can successfully apply nonviolence, but I wonder.

H

H is for Hitching

(Summer 1981)

Then let's look on the bright side: We're having an adventure, and most people live and die without being as lucky as we are.

—William Goldman, *The Princess Bride*

After our first year in college, my best friend, Greg, and I spent the summer hitchhiking across the United States and back. More than just a grand adventure, this was something each of us felt we had heard from God to undertake. During the school year we'd each spent a lot of time in prayer and on the phone with each other refining our plans for this trip. We felt we were to take no money and very few belongings and set out in complete trust in the provision of God. Our duffel bags contained as much literature and Bibles as they did clothing. We intended to witness our way across the nation.

Our adventure exceeded our expectations. The good-
ness of God was extremely evident in miracles of provision and in our encounters with the other denizens of the
open road. There were, however, at least two incidents
that could have gone very wrong.

I sent my mother postcards from the road:

August 2, 1981

*Mom, I love you, thanks for raising me in the Church and for
praying for me all those years and for always loving and forgiving
me. Right now we're riding in the backseat of a Satanist thief with a
sock full of cash (maybe $1000?) and an AWOL soldier, escapee from
a mental hospital, who renounced Christ so he could kill legally in
the Army. Our driver, the Satanist, offered us money—begged us to
take it—but we refused his $20 and explained why.* (We said we
didn't want a dime from his father, the devil, because our
Father took such great care of us.) *They both seem to be under
conviction, and I overheard the army guy say he was thinking about
Jesus again because of us.*

Mom, you sure have cool friends. Love, Brian.

Later, when I mailed the card, Greg and I were couch
surfing in the home of the friend in question, Hilda, who
added a note of her own:

*Hi Carol! What a pleasant surprise to have Brian and Greg — two
fine young men! You wouldn't believe I picked them up in the pits of
St. Louis, MO—the naiveté of youth! Glad to make the rescue. Wish
they could stay longer than a day. Looking forward to seeing you in
AA Town* (Ann Arbor) *for the* (University of Michigan Nursing
Class of '57) *reunion in October. Love, Hilda*

It all ended safely. After several hours, the men let us
out and as Greg and I were retrieving our things from
their trunk, we offered them a comic book of the Gospel

of John. Each of them took one and thanked us. Now that I'm a parent myself, I am horrified I sent my mother such postcards. At the time it didn't even cross my mind it would be terrifying for a mother to read such accounts.

It was on our westward return trip that we really got into trouble. Our clear instructions from above had been to hitchhike across the country. However, just a couple of weeks after beginning our journey, during a night's stay in a rescue mission in Billings, Montana, we'd fallen in with a group of hobos. We passed a very pleasant evening with these men of the road watching Prince Charles marry Lady Diana. It was surreal viewing the royal pomp on a tiny black and white television among the very poor. After the royal wedding, our new friends regaled us with stories of the absolute freedom of riding the rails. Greg in partic-

ular was captivated. From that night on, the idea of hopping a freight train would slip into almost every discussion about the rest of our trip.

We had gone east across the northern part of the United States, and our return was taking a more central route westward. When we reached Kansas City and stayed

My best friend, Greg.

with my mom's friend Hilda, Greg suggested we hop a freight train in the huge railroad yards there. I didn't feel perfectly okay with this plan, but I didn't want to be a dream crusher so I kept my mouth shut. We had Hilda drop us at a freeway on-ramp that was walking distance to the tracks. After she drove off, we made our way down into the great confluence of roads of steel. We found a place to hide our duffles and went among the trains looking for a westbound preparing to leave. We found one with the crew busily preparing to embark and we talked with them. They told us the train was going to stop in Las Vegas, which was perfect for us because my grandparents had moved there from Illinois. They showed us a place to hide on the train until we were safely free of the yards. They warned us about the railroad bulls, the train yard security forces who would be looking for freeloaders like us. They told us we had enough time to pick up some food and our bags and steal back aboard before they left.

We were so excited! With the crew of the train knowledgeable about and agreeable to our presence, what could go wrong? We had hidden our bags behind some dumpsters in a parking lot, and as we were retrieving them cars and sirens and very angry men suddenly surrounded us. The railroad bulls were on to us—probably alerted by the train crew. Within moments we were face down on the pavement and handcuffed. The uniformed men were screaming and cursing at us as they threw us into the back of one of the cars. The ride was short. The Santa Fe Railroad security office was practically right next door to the parking lot where they arrested us. The bulls seemed unreasonably angry with us. They pulled us out of the car by our hair, threw us against things on the way inside, and barely allowed us to answer their shouted interrogations. When they found out we were both California college students, they became even more unglued. Getting just inches from our faces they shouted, "College boy #$@&%s!," and made various slurs against our home state. The sheer rage directed at us was absolutely terrifying. The more we tried to explain ourselves, the more they despised us. When they found we were followers of Jesus, a new firestorm of abuse and actual blows were unleashed. One of them, Larry, was especially bitter against Christians. We learned he had a *crazy old uncle* who believed as we did. Surrounding us, all four bulls began to mock our faith.

At one point they left us alone in the office. Handcuffed as we were, they apparently didn't consider us a flight risk. On one of these occasions, just before leaving the room, Officer Larry asked us if we were thirsty. Thinking he was softening toward us, we told him we were. In response, he laughed cruelly and spat, "Let your God get you something to drink!" As soon as we were alone, Greg and I began to discuss our situation in whispers. We quickly came to the conclusion our dilemma was our own fault. We had changed the plan without consulting God, and had chased our own desires rather than following His word to us. We quickly bowed our heads and repented. Immediately fear left, and we felt much lighter and more hopeful. We knew our heavenly Dad had everything in hand, and we were going to be all right.

Following the prayer, we reopened our eyes, and I immediately noticed my duffel sack was within easy reach.

They'd failed to handcuff us to our chairs, so with some difficulty I was able to open my rucksack and get my bota bag (goat skin canteen) full of water. It was no great feat to squirt refreshing drinking water into Greg's mouth and then to pass him the bag so he could return the favor. I managed to return the bota to my bag and zip it shut before they returned. When they entered the office they saw two boys smiling with water dripping off our chins and wet T-shirts. Larry demanded to know who had given us water. Grinning, Greg told him, "Our God gave us something to drink." That really set the guy off into a verbally abusive rant, but from then on, he and the rest of them were toothless lions.

The steam seemed to have been let out of their rage, and after collecting some information from us and issuing dire threats should we ever chance to stray upon Santa Fe property again, they took off our handcuffs and put us back into the car. Without a word, they drove us to the same freeway on-ramp where Hilda had dropped us off that morning. As we were getting our duffel sacks out of the trunk, I quietly asked Officer Larry if we could pray for him. Looking down at the ground, he muttered, "Okay, but wait until after we drive away." As they drove off, we knelt in the gravel and offered thanks and praise to God while lifting up this angry and troubled railroad bull.

"Don't Panic."

—*The Hitchhiker's Guide to the Galaxy,* Douglas Adams

I

I is for Ice
(Spring 2009)

Some say the world will end in fire,
Some say in ice.
From what I've tasted of desire
I hold with those who favor fire.
But if it had to perish twice,
I think I know enough of hate
To say that for destruction ice
Is also great
And would suffice.

—*Fire and Ice,* Robert Frost

Perspectives on the World Christian Movement in Fayetteville, Arkansas invited me to teach. This time I would be participating in a special intensive version of the Perspectives Study Program. This class, mostly busy pastors, was working through all fifteen lessons in just a week, rather than the usual fifteen weeks. My assignment was my favorite lesson: Pioneer Church Planting.

On January 26, 2009, I flew from my home in McKinleyville, California into Tulsa, Oklahoma. The airfare had priced out hundreds of dollars cheaper into Tulsa than the local airport in Bentonville, Arkansas. The coordinator of the class instructed me to drive a rental car to Fayetteville. That morning he'd called and told me he'd changed my reservation to an SUV. This was an unusual development, as they usually rented the cheapest car available, but the weather was calling for ice storms, and he suspected I might need four-wheel-drive.

Upon arrival I picked up my SUV and drove to Fayetteville. I checked into the spacious guest quarters overlooking Razorback Stadium right on the edge of the University of Arkansas campus. By the time I'd grabbed some dinner, I was pretty tired and fell asleep soon after crawling into the queen size bed. When I woke the next morning, the weather was already threatening a storm. The class coordinator wasn't expecting me until noon as the morning was another lesson, but I decided to set out early and make sure I arrived on time. It would be fun to sit in on another lecturer and see how they taught a lesson I had delivered many times. When I arrived at the Mount Sequoya Retreat and Conference Center, the class was already halfway into Lesson 13: *The Spontaneous Multiplication of Churches*. They'dfailed to book an instructor for this class and were watching a video of my friend and mentor, Dr. George Patterson. Outside the ice storm was really picking up, and within minutes of my arrival the power failed. That was the end of the video.

I went over to the class coordinator and mentioned I could easily teach the second half of the lesson. Much relieved, he immediately accepted my offer, introduced me to the class, and I began to teach. Outside, frozen rain was falling, and falling hard. After an hour's teaching, I finished the lesson and we broke for lunch. We all dashed through the sleet across the parking lot and courtyard of the conference center to the dining hall. I enjoyed getting to know some of my students over steaming bowls of soup, and after an hour, covering our heads with whatever was handy, we dashed back to our classroom.

Without benefit of projection or amplification, I plunged old-school style into the story of what God had done with our team in launching a church planting movement in Mongolia. (If you are interested read my book: *There's a Sheep in My Bathtub; Birth of a Mongolian Church Planting Movement*, Asteroidea Books). My lesson topic, Pioneer Church Planting, is perfectly suited to telling this story which I present as a case study. That's why it's my favorite lesson to teach—because I'm basically a storyteller, and I can just tell my story. Outside the storm was really picking up in intensity as I neared the end of the first half of my talk. Suddenly, without warning, there was a tremendous crash above our heads. Boards and ceiling tiles came raining down as students dove out of the way. A hole opened above our heads with tree branches sticking through and ice and water pouring in. A frozen tree had actually fallen onto the classroom. The falling debris covered the book table. Once we ascertained no one was injured and the damaged ceiling was stable, we set about cleaning up the mess, rescuing the books, positioning trash cans to catch the water pouring down, and moving desks away from the debris field. Within twenty minutes of the sky falling, I was able to resume teaching. Just as I was getting to a particularly compelling and riveting part of my tale[3], there was another crash outside—this one accompanied by the sound of breaking glass and screeching metal. We looked out the window and saw a large tree had fallen across the parking lot. Underneath it were three cars, all more or less crushed. One looked totaled and the other two had serious scratching and broken glass. It quickly became clear the worst damaged vehicle belonged to the class coordinator. At this point I realized two things. Firstly, I was never going to be able to regain the attention of this class from what was going on outside the classroom. Secondly, if any of us were to have any hope of leaving the mountaintop we were on, we needed to start driving now.

---

[3] DVD of the author teaching Pioneer Church Planting with *The Mongolia Story* on sale at: squareup.com/market/asteroidea-books

I told the agitated students we were through for the day, and I recommended everyone try to make their way home. I tried to console the coordinator, said my goodbyes and headed for my rented SUV. My flight out was from Tulsa the next morning, and my plan had been to get up early and drive there. Now I realized I needed to drive to Tulsa immediately, if I was able, because there was no way the roads were going to be passable the next morning. I had no idea how difficult and dangerous it was going to be just getting across town to retrieve my luggage.

A thick coat of ice already covered every surface, including the roadway. I put my car in four-wheel-drive and crept out of the parking lot and onto the road down Mount Sequoya. As I was slowly making my way down the hill, I saw a truck coming toward me. When we pulled abreast we both stopped and rolled down our windows. I asked him if the road ahead was passable, and he replied it was if I was careful. There were fallen trees, but I could drive around them. As I was thanking him for the information, a tree fell directly in front of my front bumper. It fell across the bed of his pickup truck, pinning the truck to the road. He swore and got out to survey the damage. I asked him if he wanted me to get help, but he was already pulling out his cell phone. I backed up and just managed to get around the tree. As I drove across Fayetteville, it was like driving through a disaster zone. Traffic lights were out, trees and power lines littered the road, and police roadblocks complicated the maze Fayetteville had become. Not being familiar with alternate routes across the city, it took me quite a while to reach my guesthouse.

Arriving at my lodgings, I realized I had another problem. The guesthouse was on a hill and the ice was so thick, there was no way I could drive up the driveway. I had to get my luggage before I could drive to the airport, so I got out of the car and tried to walk up the driveway. This also proved impossible as my shoes provided no better traction than car tires. I ended up having to crab walk up the sloped lawn on all fours—pounding holes through the ice with my fists. Once inside I quickly gathered my things and slid my luggage down the driveway to the car. Then I sat down and slid myself down to the car. It began to sink in that I had a long way to go in some very ugly and dangerous weather.

Getting over to a freeway on-ramp with ice covering every surface was more of the same torturous, diverted, detoured driving I'd already experienced. Once on the freeway however, things were even more fraught with danger. I found I could drive no faster than 20 mph if I wanted to stay pointing straight ahead on the roadway. There were few cars on the road and there were already a number in the ditch off the side of the freeway and along the median. I had not really even gotten out of the city limits before I saw the car in front of me start to slowly spin around in circles and slide off the road. I started chanting, "Jesus" over and over. A few miles later I saw the identical scene play out with a pickup truck in my rear-view mirror. This further terrified me. I seemed to be the only driver who could stay in forward motion on the road. I was in constant prayer as I crawled towards Tulsa.

At the turn to the east that would take me through Siloam Springs and into Oklahoma, I noticed I was very low on gas. The ice storm and power outage had closed every gas station I passed. I began to pray hard there would be at least one open gas station and that it would be fairly soon. I mentioned to God the cost per gallon was, for once, not an issue. He answered quickly—I spied a lighted gas station sign. I pulled in next to a pump and found I could not open my door. A thick sheet of ice completely sealed me in my car. I held the handle and bashed my shoulder against the inside of the door but it didn't budge. The power window did work though, and I rolled it down leaving in its place a solid window of ice. I was able to break the ice and push it outward. This allowed me to reach out the window and beat on the seam where the door met the car, knocking off some of the ice that was sealing me inside. Then with some more shoulder bashing from inside I was able to escape. As I was filling my tank, the gas station attendant carefully made his way out to me across the frozen pavement. I thanked him for being open during the storm and he replied having a generator had come in handy for the first time. As he scraped my windshield of accumulated ice, he asked me if I was hungry. I replied I was mildly hungry, but could probably wait a while. He said, "I'm not sure you'll find an open restaurant between here and Tulsa. The only reason the Chinese place next door is open is because I'm providing them power. So, if you want to eat you'd better eat there." I thanked him for the advice, and after knocking off all the ice I could from my headlights, doors and wheel wells, I pulled in front of the Chinese restaurant. The number of people inside belied how few cars were on the road. The buffet quality was only average, but it had the advantage of being the only food around. Having filled both the car's tank and my own, I got back out onto the frozen road.

The trip continued to be treacherous and painstakingly slow, and although I slid from time to time, my vehicle never completely left the roadway. A little after 10 p.m., I pulled into the airport hotel the class coordinator had reserved for me. I was inexpressibly relieved to have made it, and my heart and mouth overflowed in praise to God.

The next morning I returned my rental car. My flight was listed as delayed but not cancelled. The brunt of the storm had spared Tulsa, and I would be flying home. I had survived the Great Ice Storm of 2009.

J

J is for Jerk
(1978)

Butch Cassidy: No, no, not yet. Not until me and Harvey get the
rules straightened out.
Harvey Logan: Rules? In a knife fight? No rules!
        [Butch kicks Harvey in the groin]
Butch Cassidy: Well, if there aint' going to be any rules, let's get the
fight started.

—Butch Cassidy and The Sundance Kid (film)

I'd thought the terrors of bullying were safely tucked away in my junior high past. Now that I was a sophomore at Crescenta Valley High School, I enjoyed the way my peers seemed to handle interpersonal relationships in a more mature manner not involving fisticuffs. And that's how it was, until I ran into Clay and Lee.

My English class was in a temporary building at the very edge of the school property. One afternoon, as I hurried to class, two unknown males stepped in front of me, blocking my path. One of them was my height, but far more muscular. He was swarthy with long dark brown hair and a mustache. His companion was only a tad shorter but with a much slighter build. His hair was long sunbleached blonde, parted down the middle and very straight. Mustache-Man put his hand in the center of my chest to stop me and demanded matches. I told him I didn't smoke. He contemptuously shoved me a little—just enough so I'd stumble backward a step. Surfer-Dude casually knocked my notebook out of my hand, and it popped open upon hitting the pavement. As I stooped to gather my papers, the blonde sneered, "Catch you later, $@&." He smacked the top of my head so hard I hoped he hurt his hand as they walked around me and continued on their way. I didn't know it then, but I'd just met my tormentors for the rest of the school year.

It didn't take long to find out who they were. This inseparable pair had quite a reputation. The large, dark and sinister kid was Clayton, or Clay. He had a reputation for dealing drugs and for being an all-around bad piece of work. He was a senior and thus two years older than me. His blonde sidekick was a junior, and though not exactly unattractive, Lee had a shifty and furtive way about him that was vaguely off-putting. Lee was clearly henchman to Clay's villain.

From that day on if these goons saw me before I saw them, what followed was verbal and physical abuse. I found their hatred inexplicable. I couldn't see what they got out of our relationship—certainly not money or anything concrete. I'd never done anything to warrant their enmity. It had to be they were massaging their self-images at my expense. I quickly realized I needed to keep my jerk-radar on at all times to maximize my chances of avoiding encounters with Clay and Lee. When they did catch me, what they actually did to me was not as bad as the fear growing within me—that they might one day carry out their threats of vaguely defined future harm to my person and body away from the ineffective adult supervision of the school campus. I got the impression if we ever met in a dark alley, I wouldn't make it out.

Finally June came, and I felt the undercurrent of fear I had carried for months draining away as school gave way to vacation. My Uncle Dale and Aunt Dottie and my cousins paid us a visit from Las Vegas, Nevada, a six-hour drive from our Glendale, California home. I always loved it when they stayed with us, having always been close to my cousin David. On their first full day with us, Dale and I went out to get sandwiches for everyone at *The Pickle Barrel*, a deli in Montrose, California with sandwiches named after TV and movie stars. We found a place to park almost a block away from the restaurant. As we were crossing the street, my blood ran cold. Lee was skateboarding with four other teens right in front of The Pickle Barrel! My uncle Dale is a huge man. Well over 6 feet tall, he's also quite large in every other dimension. I quickly scurried behind him so his bulk would hide me from Lee's gaze.

It didn't work. Lee had already seen me coming. He skillfully rode his skateboard down the sidewalk and cornered so suddenly he almost grazed me. Just as he passed, he spit directly in my face. I quickly used the short sleeve of my Hang 10 shirt to wipe his saliva from my cheek. My uncle gave no indication he had seen what happened, and that was a relief. Lee skated back to his friends. The skaters' mocking laughter followed me through the doors of The Pickle Barrel.

After standing in line and placing the sandwich orders, Dale ordered us each a soda, and we sat in a booth to wait. They were busy so the sandwiches were going to be a while. My desire for concealment was obvious as I carefully sat out of sight from the window.

"What's your deal with that kid?" my uncle asked.

"What do you mean? What kid?" I stammered.

"That longhair who just spit in your face." Uncle Dale often seemed all-knowing. He has the gift of uncanny perception. It served him well in his long career teaching elementary P.E. in Las Vegas. This wasn't the first time he'd annoyed me with this ability.

"Why'd you let him get away with that?"

"Because he's scary and always hangs out with this total thug."

My uncle studied the skaters outside the window and asked, "Which one is the thug?"

"His name is Clay, and he's not with him now."

"Then get out there and make it crystal clear to this punk he doesn't want to spit at you again."

It was clear my uncle was not asking me, but rather telling me, what I needed to do. My lack of a father had meant that over the years Uncle Dale would occasionally say and do things to fill the void. This was one of those times, and I couldn't see a way to refuse. The hardest part was simply sliding out of the booth and standing up. As I forced myself to walk toward the door, my fear drained away.

I walked out and made a bee-line to Lee who was doing tricks about 10 yards from his friends. His startled look at my resolute approach gave me whatever confidence I was still lacking. Without further warning, I delivered a roundhouse punch into the side of his face. He fell off his board and his butt hit the hard sidewalk. Before he could react, I used both hands to grab his shirt collar and yank him to his feet. I pulled his face in just 4 inches from mine. Tears were already welling in his eyes. Unconsciously and dramatically, I managed to channel Clint Eastwood and growled, "Nobody spits on a Hogan." I continued to hold Lee in position while I waited for some acknowledgment—a nod or some words—that he'd received the message. Instead, I felt a sharp pressure just above my belly button. Lee hissed, "Let go. I swear I'll stab you!"

Suddenly, the poking I was feeling in my belly had a context. I looked down and saw an open switchblade in Lee's hand pressed quite convincingly and painfully against my stomach. My thoughts seemed to come at the speed of sound. Even more terrifying than the thought of a knife plunging into my stomach was the knowledge that if I backed down now I'd be this boy's designated victim for the rest of high school. With no discernible pause, I answered, "Go ahead. Push it in. I swear before you have time to pull it out, I'll be smashing your face over and over into the sidewalk. No matter what happens to me you'll never be the same."

We stood there, frozen, for what seemed an eternity, but was probably only seconds. Finally, *the other guy blinked.* With discernable fear in his voice, Lee begged, "Just let me go, dude."

"Not until I know I am done with you and Clay for good. I don't even exist for you from now on."

"Okay, okay. Be cool! Just let go," he pleaded.

I released Lee and he backed away. It was as if a stasis spell suddenly released both of us. We began to notice what was going on around us. The other skaters were just a few feet away and hadn't missed a word. They were smirking, and I heard them mocking Lee as I walked back into the restaurant. As I rejoined my uncle, neither of us said a word. Uncle Dale simply grinned.

I have no idea what, or even if, Lee told Clay, but they never approached me again. I wasn't even sure they were still in contact. In fact, Clay never graduated, but he was finished with school, and I never laid eyes on him again. I did see Lee from time to time on campus, but he always seemed to have pressing business in another direction when he saw me.

K

K is for Kidnapping

(Spring 1971)

Author's Note: This story has been modified in this edition for a wide audience of all ages. Still rated PG, as some thematic elements may require parental guidance for younger readers. The full and unexpurgated version of "K is for Kidnapping" may be read online at AsteroideaBooks.com.

I was nine years old and doing my best to ignore pangs of guilt. I was ditching choir practice at Magnolia Park Methodist Church and hurrying home to enjoy an afterschool snack with Patty Jean, our live-in childcare. Patty Jean was a close family friend from my mom's hometown of Blue Island, Illinois, and was staying with us while she attended college. This pretty, Jesus-freak hippy girl traded room and board for watching over me while my mother worked at Children's Hospital. I had my first crush on Patty Jean and was trying to get her to promise to wait until I was old enough to marry her (there was only

The author in choir gear with Patti Jean. No wonder I ditched!

an eleven year difference!). This probably had a lot to do with my decision that day to skip choir.

Our home at 214 N. California Street in Burbank, California, was only one long downhill block from my school, R. L. Stevenson Elementary. It was usually an uneventful walk, aside from having to scurry past our street's "haunted" house at the top of the hill. This neglected place looked more like the set for *The Addams Family* rather than any of the other houses in our quiet neighborhood. It produced delicious thrills of fear in all of us kids on California Street. My house was far down the hill on the opposite side of the street, but I dared myself to walk on the right-hand, or scary, side.

Perhaps it was my brief burst of speed past that house that attracted his attention. Maybe there were foul spirits operating in that place. At any rate, I had just made it past the fearful house when a beige 1963 Ford Galaxy pulled to a stop next to me. A young man leaned over and spoke to me through the open passenger side window.

"Hey, kid. I have a mini-bike in the trunk and am looking for the trails where I can ride it. Do you know where they are?"

We were facing down the street and the scrub filled hills of Griffith Park were clearly visible straight ahead of us. I didn't know anything about motorcycles or mini-bikes or anything motorized, but, ever helpful, I guessed, "The trails are up there in Griffith Park," and I pointed toward the hill.

"Thanks!" He replied, with more seeming gratitude than my ignorant help warranted. "Would you like to come along and ride with me?"

"No" I quickly responded. I knew better than to accept rides with strangers. I started walking again.

Pulling up alongside me, he asked, "Where are you headed?

"Home. It is right down there," as I pointed out our house in the distance.

The scene of the crime - looking down California St. towards my house.

"Hop in. I'll give you a ride home."

"I can walk. It's real close."

"No. Let me pay you back for the directions you gave me. Just get in and you will be home in a few seconds."

His logic seemed sound and I felt like I'd be impolite rejecting his kind offer, so I got in. He started down the hill. When we came to my house I told him "Here it is," but he just kept driving without a word, right past my house. As we drove toward the intersection, just 266 feet beyond our house, I realized this was a kidnapping. I instantly had a vision of myself sitting in choir practice, where everyone would think I was, and bitterly regretted my wicked decision to play the truant. As he paused at the intersection of N. California and W. Alameda Ave., preparing to make a right turn, I could see all the costumed "Let's Make a Deal!" hopefuls lined up across the street in front of NBC Studios, and briefly thought of getting out and screaming for help. My abductor read my mind and clenched his hand on my shoulder. Hope died.

I was terrified. The only thing I could do was pray. Since I'd offended God by refusing to sing to Him, He was my only appeal. I silently called out to Him.

"God, I'm so sorry. Please save me from this man. Please, please, please. Help me! Get me home!"

As we turned onto Alameda, racking sobs began to push up from my chest. More tears than I thought possible began to spout from my eyes, and I began to wail like I'd never done before. I had no idea what was happening to me, but God had just given me the spiritual gift of uncontrollable crying!

The man told me to shut up. I could not. I only cried harder. He repeated his demand several times with increasing menace in his voice as we drove down that busy street.. I wanted to comply, frightened of what he might do if I didn't, but I was helpless before the supernatural gush of inconsolable weeping. He turned left onto N. Hollywood Way and began a torrent of verbal abuse as he cursed me and threatened with some words I had never heard before and just about every word I knew and had tried out—with a mouth scrubbed out with soap as my payment. I put my hands over my mouth to stifle my sobs but it was as useful as trying to stop the flow from a fire hose with your hand.

He turned right on W. Olive Ave. and drove a half mile. As we crossed the bridge over the concrete-jacketed Los Angeles River, my abductor pulled out a Bowie knife and held it against my throat.

"Quit crying! I haven't done anything to you, but if you don't stop I swear I will cut your head off and make you stop!"

I redoubled my efforts to squelch my squalling. I was trying to save my life. But my desperate attempts to silence myself only resulted in adding violent and loud hiccups punctuating my tearful lamentations.

As we turned left onto Forest Lawn Drive, the beginning of the perimeter road around Griffith Park, I could see the channel of the Los Angeles River on the left side and chaparral scrub covering the hills to my right. I knew that just ahead lay Forest Lawn Memorial Park, a sprawling and typically Californian cemetery. I had been there many times to see the faux historic churches, Liberty Bell, mural, Crown Jewel replicas, and the famous graves. Now I had the unwelcome thought thrust into my brain that I might very soon be taking up residency in a grave there.

As the misplaced verdant green of the cemetery came into view amidst the unrelenting dry greys and browns of the surrounding hills, my kidnapper lowered the knife and gripped the wheel to turn right onto a dirt road. We went up the hill about 200 feet and pulled off into a stand of dry bushes. We were exactly across from the famous Hollywood sign on the opposite side of the hill. Stopping there, he parked and came around to my door. I was bawling as loudly and moistly as ever as he pulled my arm and forced me into a clearing in the brush, screened from prying eyes on the road below.

"It's all right. You're fine. Stop your stupid crying!" the tall thin man demanded again, throwing out a filthy blanket pierced with foxtail burrs onto the dry sandy ground.

I tried again, but with no more success than before. My shoulders wracked with sobs and periodic hiccups. His face glared rage and disgust with my unseemly display. I was sure my time was extremely limited as I noticed he'd replaced the knife in its belt sheath.

He next demanded that I lie down on the blanket. Howling with more force than I'd ever managed in my life, I complied. I had no conception of what he intended, but something in me screamed that this was really wrong.

He stood there for what seemed like an hour and was probably less than a minute, looking down on a weeping nine year old boy. Then he yanked me to my feet by my arm and, with a fresh torrent of cursing, pushed me toward the car.

"Get in!" he yelled, wrenching open the door. I quickly complied and slid into the passenger seat, willing myself to be silent and invisible. I was unsuccessful, as my unworldly wailing continued unabated. This bawling completely astounded me, and I had no idea where it was all coming from.

My kidnapper stomped around and slid back behind the wheel and started up the car. We raised quite a cloud behind us as he tore back to the paved road. Even though I could see that we were returning the way we had come, and sensed that I had escaped something really horrible, I still wept loudly.

He was silent as he drove us back across the river into Burbank. The only thing he said was, "You need to keep your mouth shut about this, okay? If you tell anyone I will come and kill you with my knife. I know which house you live in." Then he fell back into brooding silence. When we pulled back onto Alameda, he reached across me and opened the passenger door. We were driving slowly in the right lane and the curb was sailing by just four or five feet away. I was looking out the open door with alarm, having never before been in a moving car with a door open. Without a word, he viciously shoved my shoulder and sent me toppling out of his car and onto the pavement. I rolled to the curb, and leapt to my feet and starting running toward home. I never gave a backward glance. I don't remember when exactly the weeping stopped, but it may have been immediate upon my ejection onto the road. It had continued unbroken from the moment I had called out to God for help, until I was free. As I ran, I took stock. Aside from minor road rash, I was physically unharmed.

I burst into our front door, screaming for Patty Jean. She ran into the living room and I ran into her arms. Then I started crying again, but these tears were natural. I poured out the story between sobs and Patty Jean held and comforted me, then led me into the kitchen, and while wiping my face with a wet washcloth, told me that we were going straight to the Burbank Police Department.

As we were heading out the door toward her Ford Maverick parked in front of the house, the phone rang. Patty Jean ran back in to answer it. It was my mother asking if everything was alright. Patty simply told her, "Brian was kidnapped but he is fine. I'm taking him to the Burbank Police Department now. Meet us there." My mom calmly replied, "Okay. I will see you in twenty minutes."

Just recently I found out the rest of that story. I was visiting my "Aunt" Marcia who still lives in Burbank (my mother died in 2011). Marcia went to nursing school with my mother at the University of Michigan, and they had come out to California together and were roommates as they worked at Children's hospital. They ended up marrying best friends (both of whom abandoned their families after fathering children) and were still very close. When I asked Marcia if she remembered my kidnapping, she said, "Yes, because I was with your mother as she found out you'd been kidnapped." I'd never heard this and asked her to relate the story.

"Your mom and I were in a nursing supervisors' meeting at the hospital. Suddenly I saw her smile disappear and her face blanch. Carol immediately stood and left the room without a word. No one said a word, but puzzled looks passed around the table. A few minutes passed and she returned, swept her papers into a folder and announced, 'There is an emergency with Brian and I have to leave.' We had no idea what caused this completely unprecedented behavior, but we just pitched in and covered for her the few hours remaining in the day. It wasn't until the next day that she filled me in. Of course, I was shocked about what you endured, but the thing that really amazed me was what had happened with your mom. She told me that in our meeting she had suddenly had a powerful and undeniable impression that something was wrong with her son, and she rushed out to call home. She had reached Patty Jean just a moment before she shut the door and left the house. You know the rest of the story. She paused only to grab her things and tell us she was leaving and then rushed to meet you at the police station."

I was amazed at this story that I had never heard, and Marcia simply said, "You and your mother were alone in the world and only had each other. That caused a powerful bond where she could sense your distress even eight miles away."

The only things I remember from the rest of that day were a Detective Coyle asking me lots of questions about the man, his car, and everything he said and did, while writing down all my words, helping a really cool police artist draw a picture of my kidnapper's face (I really felt like a bad describer, but the drawing later helped Det. Coyle to break the case), and my mom arriving and wrapping me in her arms. Those were the best tears of the day.

After all the excitement, life returned to normal, at least on the outside. No one talked to me about what had happened, and I got the impression that it was a shameful secret. Inside, I was still very frightened, not all the time . . . I was a pretty happy and optimistic hyperactive little boy . . . but at night. I would lie awake after my mom tucked me in and prayed with me. "Now I lay me down to sleep. I pray the Lord my soul to keep. If I should die before I wake, I pray the Lord my soul to take." I'd never before given a thought to the words of my memorized prayer, but now the dying part seemed a real possibility. He'd threatened to kill me if I told on him, and that was exactly what I'd done. I'd shown him my house, and he was out there on the loose somewhere. My terrors were exacerbated greatly by inputs both contemporary and of a literary nature.

For one thing, the Manson Family and their grisly murders were absolutely dominating the news. They'd perpetrated all these horrors within a 15 mile radius of our house. The Manson girls' death sentences were issued only two weeks before my abduction, and Charles Manson himself was awaiting trial. My bedroom window faced the street, and I'd already been imagining killers coming through it with knives for two years. Now my fears were reality. My kidnapper had threatened to come and kill me if I squealed. These terrors completely replaced my earlier worries about the monster in my closet.

Compounding these local news terrors, came *The Adventures of Tom Sawyer*. A month after my ordeal, I flew to spend the summer in Illinois with my Papa and Nana Anderson. In their closet I had discovered the *Reader's Digest Condensed Version of* this book and had devoured it in a single sitting. It was instantly my favorite book and Tom and Huck were imaginary friends that would walk to and from school with me throughout fourth grade. However, the scene where Tom has to testify in court against Injun Joe despite threats the villain had made to kill him if he talked, hit way too close to home. I was sure, just like Tom in the courtroom, an assassin was stalking me.

As I flew back to Los Angeles International by myself, the danger ahead filled my thoughts. It didn't help that my mom had to take me to the Burbank Police Department right after I landed. Van Nuys police had picked up a man matching the police drawing I helped create. He was a suspect in the kidnapping of a number of boys in Van Nuys and a couple more in Burbank. The Burbank police were waiting impatiently for me to identify him from a photo lineup, so they could make their case, and my long summer vacation out-of-state frustrated them. Shown the table full of pictures, I recognized him immediately with a shudder. This was the face in my nightmares. I found out years later that Officer Coyle immediately drove over and arrested this man at his parents' Van Nuys home.

Relieved as I was by the knowledge that he was safely behind bars, a new terror loomed on my horizon. The police made it clear when the time came for his trial, I would have to get into the witness box and identify him in court. I knew all about this because my mom was a *Perry Mason* fan and I would watch this TV courtroom drama with her so that I could watch *Gilligan's Island* and *The Flying Nun.* (I was a fickle lover and had by this time given up on Patty Jean—her engagement didn't help—and transferred my undying love to Sally Fields, who played Sister Bertrille.) The prospect of having to face this monster in court—just as Tom had faced Injun Joe—began to haunt my dreams.

The day inevitably came. Patty Jean and I received subpoenas to testify in Municipal Court of Burbank on October 14th, 1971 in the case of People of the State of California vs. Thomas L————. (I didn't know any of these particulars or even his name until 2013 when my stepdad sent me some of my mom's papers, and I found the subpoena.) All I knew that day was I was missing class to go to court. And that *he* would be there and find out I had told on him.

My teacher got a note from the office and told me to go to the principal. My mom collected me there and drove me to the courthouse. Patty Jean wasn't there. I assume that my mom made her excuse to the court as Patty Jean no longer lived with us, and her actual knowledge of the case was really no more than my mother's. (Two months earlier Patty had moved into her own apartment nearby and married. I could walk to her house, but rarely did.)

The only actual memories I retain of that day in court were twenty-one boys and their parents waiting to testify in the hall outside the courtroom. None of us kids spoke at all, though some of the parents had short furtive conversations with other parents. I understood how the other boys felt. I didn't want to make eye contact with them any more than they wanted to with me. The other thing burned into my memory was the bailiff taking me into the courtroom and leading up into the witness box. He'd instructed my mother to remain outside in the hallway. Marcia later told me Mom was furious about this. I have a single and very vivid memory of the District Attorney asking me to point out the man who had kidnapped me. I was forced to look at him—something I'd been avoiding—and as he glared hatefully at me, I had to raise my suddenly leaden arm and point at him sitting at the table in front and below me. Only my buddy, Tom Sawyer, could understand how scary this was for me.

And then it was over. The bailiff led me out. We drove home. And I don't remember anyone ever talking about it to me again. I thought about it a lot at first, remembering the threat and hate in his eyes, but kids are resilient, and I have always been abnormally optimistic—"a miserable enthusiast". The thoughts and fears diminished and eventually almost completely disappeared.

Years later, as I contemplated writing a book about my many miraculous close calls, I immediately thought of how God had saved me through geysers of tears during my kidnapping. About six months later I received that yellowed old subpoena, and the search was on. I at last had a name to attach to my fearful and foggy memories. Thomas L———.

While in Los Angeles for a teaching engagement, I scheduled in a couple days for research. I planned to scour the court archives, police files, D.A.'s records, anything on the case that they would give me access to as a victim. I looked up old Burbank newspapers on microfilm at the library, made calls all over, and ran into one dead end after another. I even spoke to a Burbank cop who actually called in to the station to try and help pry lose the files, but no luck. They destroyed records ten years after the trial.

I was unwilling to give up. I'd found the perpetrator's home address on an online criminal registry, and I began to think that my kidnapper might be the only primary source of information left around. I decided to pay Thomas L——— a visit.

My GPS took me right to the shabby house in a declining Van Nuys neighborhood. Almost swallowed by overgrown vegetation, the residence seemed to be cowering behind two semi-derelict RVs in the driveway and an old panel van curbside. As I got out of my rental car, I saw him coming out of the RV's side door. I walked over to this disheveled old man in a tee shirt and house slippers and stuck out my hand.

"Hi. I'm Brian."

We shook and he replied warily, "I'm Tom."

I had not thought this through and had no idea what to say next. I just blurted out, "We met in 1971 in Burbank when you picked me up on my way home from school."

He began to reposition his feet as he contemplated his chances of getting inside his front door before I could catch him.

"I'm not angry. I am not here for vengeance, and I have no desire to hurt you. Don't worry! I just want to talk and ask you some questions."

He seemed to relax minimally. "That was a long time ago. I did time for those crimes. I am very sorry for what I did to you and the other boys. There is no excuse. That was a terrible thing to do to anyone. I'm very sorry."

I acknowledged his apology, which he repeated three times over the next several hours. We stood in his yard and talked for a long while. I asked if we could get out of the sun, and he suggested my car. He said he needed to change into his shoes and use the restroom, and went inside the house, shutting the door behind him. I went and sat in my car with the air conditioning on, but, to be honest, I thought I'd lost him. I was surprised to see him about ten minutes later. We went on talking in the car, and eventually I persuaded him to let me take him out to lunch. Over the course of three hours I found out so many things. His first crime was arson at age nine. He tried to torch a Catholic Church where he was in school. A priest had abused Tom for weeks, and his response was arson. Charged and convicted in juvenile court, no one believed him about the priest. Not even his own mother. After his release, Tom's parents put him in a nearby military school where he was tormented by the older boys. At seventeen he got his first violent crime conviction. At twenty-one he kidnapped me and the other boys. He told me he felt that all the boys were at least "going along with it" and "he didn't force anyone." I took issue with this and told him how threatened I had felt and about my tears. He said that must have been what made him let me go.

My testimony and that of others sent him first to prison and then to Atascadero State Mental Hospital. Eventually labelled a Mentally Disordered Offender and released, Tom took up painting cars and, in lieu of advertising, sprayed acid on new cars to generate business. Some of the acid blew into motorists' faces. Tom returned to prison for gross bodily injury by chemical means. He became embittered against his lawyer for failing to defend him properly. When released he put skills learned in prison to work, counterfeiting and passing fake currency. His purchase of special currency grade paper attracted Treasury Department attention. This time, in addition to a prison sentence, they confiscated his car. This further enraged Tom against the system. He began sending threating letters through the mail to fire departments and others, in-cluding his erstwhile lawyer. He threatened to burn Los Angeles to the ground. This was during a bad 1994 fire season, and Malibu and other hilly areas were soon ablaze. The letters, all signed The Fedbuster, led back to Tom, whom the FBI arrested (for using the mail to threaten, not for arson) and sentenced to Terminal Island Federal Penitentiary. After his eventual release, there was another arrest in a police sting operation on Santa Monica

Blvd., but, by this time, Tom's crime spree had largely played out.

He told me he has been alone for years and volunteers to feed the homeless at a local church. I asked if he was a believer in Jesus, and he affirmed that he was. He again apologized for kidnapping me. He said that he didn't remember me specifically as a victim, though he remembered my name from court. I suggested that because my torrent of emotion had frustrated his aim—by destroying his pretense that I was "going along with it," he had likely picked up another Burbank boy soon after dumping me. That one he probably remembered. I was happy to be forgettable.

At the end of our time I looked him in the eyes and told him, "Tom, I forgive you. I don't hold anything against you. You need to sort it all out with God, but since He is the one empowering me to forgive, I know that you won't find it difficult with Him." I told him several times to make sure he understood. He thanked me, and we shook hands and I blessed him. Then I drove away.

Two weeks later, back in Los Angeles, I drove by to give him a copy of my book, *There's a Sheep in my Bathtub*, pray with him, and ask him a few more questions. He was not home, so I left the book and a note. Later Tom emailed me, thanked me for the book, and invited me to ask my questions. I was able to confirm the memories offered here. So the story isn't over. It's exciting to see the kingdom of God at work.

Bad people are good soil for the gospel.

L

L is for Lost

(Summer 1968)

I once was lost, but now I'm found.

—John Newton, *Amazing Grace*

My mother and I went camping with my father's parents during what the papers were calling the *Summer of Love*. Nana and Papa Hogan weren't much for roughing it, but they took any excuse to be with their six year old grandson, so off we went to a Forest Service campground near Idyllwild, California. While the adults were setting up camp, I took off to scout out the area. It was not at all clear where the campground ended and the wilderness began—at least not to me. I started down a likely looking trail and soon encountered a boy, of maybe 10 years, also out exploring. Tired of being alone, he was more than willing to overlook the age difference and join me. Our trail eventually ended in a ravine, and we picked our way down into it. As we scrambled over and around boulders, we lost track of time.

Meanwhile, back at the campsite, my family had noted my absence. Mom, a pediatric nurse and expert on all-things-Brian, didn't panic easily. My grandparents, on the other hand, went straight into *he's-lost-forever-and-what-ever-will-we-do?* mode. My mother did her best to organize a search of the campground as Nana and Papa ran off in opposite directions frantically calling my name. Quickly deputized, other adult campers joined the search. It didn't take long to determine I had left the developed camping area. A mother from the far side of the campground revealed her son was missing as well. The worried searchers added him to the missing list. As those calling our names fanned farther out and away from the campground, anxiety began to spike.

An hour and a half passed with no sign of either lost boy. Someone drove to the ranger station to alert the authorities and get them involved in the search. By this point my mother had joined the ranks of the deeply worried, and my grandparents were in danger of cardiac arrest. Suddenly, someone came running back into the campground dragging my companion behind. The ten-year-old's frantic parents immediately deluged the boy with hugs, tears, and questions. Stunned and confused by the uproar surrounding him, he readily admitted to having been with me. When questioned regarding my whereabouts, the boy claimed ignorance. He told the frantic adults he'd retraced his steps and headed back to camp because he was afraid of getting in trouble. I'd wanted to keep going, so he'd left me. After all, he wasn't my babysitter.

The searchers who'd returned in response to the shouts of, "Found him!" plunged back into the search. Dusk was coming on, and the thought of daylight failing soon added to the frantic determination to locate me. Papa Hogan hadn't returned when the other boy was located. He was about three-quarters of a mile from the campground and searching along a rock-strewn ravine. As he rounded a bend he chanced to pull his eyes upward, away from the unstable surface his feet were navigating, and froze in horror at the sight above him. A nine-inch water pipe spanned the top of the ravine from rim to rim. Above and parallel to the pipe ran a steel cable helping suspend the pipe below. In the middle of this span, twenty feet above the tumbled white rocks of the ravine floor, his six-year-old grandson stood—small tennis shoes on the swaying pipe and fingers clutching the cable for balance.

"BRIAN!!" Erupted from Papa's throat louder than any sound I'd ever heard from him. I was so startled at this sudden bellow from below that I missed my step. Only my death grip on the steel cable saved me from a plunge. I quickly got both feet back onto the pipe. Recovering, I called down, "Hi Papa. Found a bridge."

Terrified at my near fall and trying hard not to scare me again, he begged, "Brian, stay right where you are. Don't move!"

I loved my grandpa, and on the very rare occasion he told me what to do I always obeyed him. But this was puzzling. I couldn't stay in the middle of the bridge. I needed to keep going to reach the other side. Why did he want me to stay up here?

Apparently, following what must've been different trails of thought, Papa Hogan came to the same conclusion. He couldn't get up to the bridge and come out and get me. He couldn't leave me there in the middle and go all the way back to bring help. I would need to complete what I had started. He would need to not die of heart failure while I did it. After some indecision, he told me I should carefully keep moving toward the end of the bridge. This made more sense to me, so I quickly complied.

When I reached the rim of the ravine and stepped off the pipe, my grandfather yelled up for me to sit down and wait for him. He sternly forbade me to move from that spot. Painstakingly, he backtracked to a place where he could make his way up to the gully's rim. When he reached me, he grabbed me into a hug tight enough to feel a bit like discipline. Papa Hogan had never laid a hand on me in anger; indeed the word *no* didn't seem to be in his vocabulary. I was more than a little shocked. Some of the torrent of words he poured over me indicated he might be angry with me for the first time. It was clear he was as frightened as he'd ever been. He told me I'd taken several years off of his life which I found horrifying and impossible at the same time. After a while, he was calm enough to take my hand and lead me back to the campsite. After all, there was still a search to call off.

Our reappearance in the campground ignited more of these mixed-up confusing adult reactions. I remember hugs from Mom and Nana Hogan with tears pouring down their cheeks. Nana was sobbing so hard she got the hiccups. This was funny, but somehow I knew better than to laugh. Mom made it clear I was in the doghouse and punishment was coming. I received a sentence of picnic table grounding until further notice. After everyone else drifted away, my mother and my grandparents had an almost heated discussion about packing up and heading immediately back to Burbank. My mother eventually prevailed and talked them into finishing out the camping trip, insisting what had happened was typical behavior for boys, and especially so for me. Doctors finally diagnosed my Attention Deficit Disorder when I started the second grade, but my mother had already realized what she was dealing with. She tucked me into my sleeping bag in our yellow and green Sears tent immediately after dinner. My punishment was to miss out on the campfire and s'mores. Tearfully, I consoled myself that I'd get some the next night for sure.

I'd like to say the rest of the trip went well for all concerned, but this is a non-fiction title. I will recount another near-death adventure from the same trip in "W is for Whirlpool."

Papa and Nana Hogan supervising the author's picnic table incarceration

M

M is for Mosquito
(2014)

This means we are running around the world telling people (by our actions not our words), "Our God can get you to heaven but He can't cure your malaria because He apparently does not know or care or have power in that sphere." Thus, being invisibly and unconsciously saddled with this theology, we can't do anything about malaria either, and since very few others are concerned, we should just pray about it, help those who already have it, and let it go at that. That is, for our part we pray, but rely on Jewish or secular doctors and researchers to do the rest. Our Christianity does not call us to fight the origins of disease, not since Augustine.

—Ralph D. Winter, *Eleven Frontiers of Mission, IJFM Fall 2003*

June 12th, 2014. I'd only been home from Africa for five days.

The results of my training trip to Mozambique were nothing short of spectacular. A protracted and difficult route involving airplanes, overnight layovers, multiple borders, taxi, ferry, and motorcycle, had eventually deposited me in a tiny village of mud huts in the center of an island in the mouth of the wide Zambezi River. I found, eagerly awaiting my arrival, a group of students from four African countries and eight people groups already well along in their School of Frontier Mission. They were preparing to work among five unreached people groups: three in Mozambique, one in Zambia, and another in Somalia. During my single week of training translated into Portuguese, these eager Africans managed to soak up two weeks of church planting training. We went mornings, afternoons, and sometimes into the evenings. It was both grueling and glorious!

While on the island, I was careful to slather myself with insect repellent and, when possible, retreat under my bed's mosquito netting in the evening. I hadn't managed to secure antimalarials as I rushed to pack for this trip, so these precautions were quite important.

However, on one occasion my plans went awry. There was no cell signal in the village and therefore no way to receive email. We would walk about a half mile to a sweet spot on a narrow trail between rice fields where for some reason signal bars would suddenly appear on our phones. We would sit alongside the trail, trying to stay out of the way of motorcycles and bicycles, everyone checking email on their cell phones. I even purchased airline tickets there to visit a friend near George, South Africa, to occupy a two night layover on my way home. On one particular visit to the *Trailside Internet Café* dusk began to fall, and my friends were all still online. Though I was aware of my need to return to the safety of my netting, I had no idea which of the many twisting trails led back to our village. I politely waited for everyone to finish and swatted the evening mosquitoes that began to come out. It really wasn't that long, but they did get a few good bites in.

I arrived back in Arkansas two days later. After being home for less than a week, I was surprised when the attack began. I was talking with a friend on the phone and all of a sudden shaking chills and aches wracked my entire body. I experienced an overwhelming desire to become quickly horizontal. I barely faked my way through the rest of the phone call and went directly to bed. I was deathly ill and near unable to move! For some reason, right away, I had a sense I'd contracted malaria.

What a blessing from God to have a close friend who is also a doctor! We immediately called Dr. James Dunn who, after asking a lot of questions to rule out a flu that was making the rounds, concurred with my diagnosis of malaria. He prescribed Mefloquine, called it in to Walgreens, and Louise rushed down the hill to pick some up. While she was out my men's prayer group left their meeting and all came over to surround me in prayer.

This attack could hardly have come at a worse time. It was Father's Day, our 30th Wedding Anniversary, our son was across the hall and going through a crisis of faith following the disappointment of the cancellation of his Backpacker's Discipleship Training School, our yard was completely torn up by workmen digging trenches to stop our foundation from being undermined by groundwater, and Louise was gone for 8 to 12 hours stretches delivering three babies in one week!

I took Mefloquine for two days and, after an initial one-day improvement, I soon was flat on my back again. When I started peeing blood, the threat level went up several notches. Louise researched online and found that I had just moved from *Simple* to *Complicated* Malaria. At one point the shakes and muscle contractions were so severe, five blankets were not enough to keep me warm. Even in the Arkansas summer heat, Louise climbed in bed and held me to try to stop my shaking. My body's thermostat seemed to have gone completely haywire.

We were soon back on the phone with the doctor. Mefloquine was obviously ineffective against the strain of malaria I had picked up. We were shooting in the dark attempting to find out what would kill this pernicious parasite. Dr. Dunn next prescribed Doxycycline. Again Louise rushed out to pick up my new medication. After two doses and no relief, I had an idea. I remembered a friend and coworker from our days in Mongolia. Patrick Brunson was a pharmacist for the Southern Baptist IMB mission agency. After leaving Mongolia, he practiced for years in Tanzania. It occurred to me if anyone was familiar with effective treatments for East African malarial strains it was Patrick. However, in the 18 years since we had last been together in Ulaanbaatar, I'd only spoken to him once.

I'd tracked Patrick down several years before and knew he was now living in Alabama. I called his number and was pleasantly surprised when he answered on the second ring. I explained the situation, and the first thing he told

me was to stop taking Doxycycline. It was completely ineffective against the strain of parasite swimming in my
blood. In fact, it could increase the resistance to medication. Patrick told me he had just lost a friend in Alabama
to undiagnosed malaria. He stressed the danger I was in
without proper treatment. Giving me the name of the preferred medication for the region in coastal Mozambique
in which I contracted malaria, Patrick extracted a promise
that I'd call him back about how I progressed.

We called Dr. Dunn and filled him in on what we'd
learned from Dr. Brunson. James said he'd check around
and see if the drug was available anywhere locally. After
an hour, he called me back and said he'd been unable to
find anyone with a supply of the drug, but his research had
revealed Malarone would be just as effective. We were familiar with Malarone, having taken it while we lived in
Tanzania. To prevent malaria, the dosage was one tablet
weekly, but to cure it I'd need to take a higher dose. Dr.
Dunn called in a prescription, and Louise set off to fill it.
Before she returned, Patrick Brunson called and said we
should consider Malarone, as it would probably be easier
to get and would be just as effective. Through Facebook, I
was able to contact the school director from Mozambique.
Justino suggested the same drug Patrick had suggested and
mentioned Malarone as an alternative. Talk about confir-
mation!

Within a day of starting the course of Malarone I was
feeling significantly better. On the sixth day of my illness,
I was able to get out of bed and even get outside a little. By
the next day I felt completely healed except for a bout of

sweating that occurred every morning for another week. I get a lot of questions as to whether I will suffer re-occurrences. My doctor assures me this won't be a problem in my case. God is good—all the time!

N

N is for Nail

(Summer 1971)

*... he could go fishing or swimming when and where he chose, and
stay as long as it suited him; nobody forbade him to fight; he could
sit up as late as he pleased; he was always the first boy that went
barefoot in the spring and the last to resume leather in the fall; he
never had to wash, nor put on clean clothes; he could swear
wonderfully. In a word, everything that goes to make life precious
that boy had.*

—Mark Twain, *Tom Sawyer*

oes any boy realize how close to perfection the
summer of his ninth year comes? I spent the
summer of 1971, like most summers, with my
grandparents in Blue Island, Illinois. My mother worked
full time at Children's Hospital of Los Angeles and needed
help with childcare when I was out of school. I was a very
active (okay, hyperactive) nine-year-old and my mother's

parents, Jim and Alice, provided an amazing amount of stability for me with their loving and firm parenting style. These summer visits were full of nature and learning, museums and road trips, and once, summer camp.

In front of my cabin at Foundation Farm Camp arrival—in clean clothes.

The Foundation Farm Camp in Palos Hills, Illinois was a two-week experience that included all the classic summer camp activities plus the opportunity to care for farm animals. I was in heaven. I had new friends, adventures, singing, stories, archery, feeding the hogs, everything needed for childhood bliss. The supervision wasn't very stringent—the hands-off approach allowed me to wear the same pair of clothes for two solid weeks with no nagging from nosy counselors. Did I mention it was boy heaven?

Upon my return, Nana Alice simply threw my filthy rags away.

The counselors were really fun and unpredictable. One night they took us to sleep out in the nearby cemetery— the kind my grandfather always referred to as a *marble orchard* with lots of standing stones and monuments. They told us horrific ghost stories, of course, the most memorable of which had to do with the large monument that formed a kind of a headboard for where we had placed our bed rolls.

This large marble obelisk had a single word upon it: Butcher.

Apparently, around the turn-of-the-century Mr. Butcher, a well-to-do businessman and his family, lived in a large home not far from this very cemetery. One morning this respectable man rose from his bed, shaved his face, and calmly and inexplicably proceeded to horribly murder his wife and two children with his shaving razor. The family's maid arrived for work and entered the home just in time to see him completing his grisly handiwork. Screaming, she perished from fright on the spot. Her screams did result in his apprehension by the authorities while still at the scene covered in the blood of his family. In the subsequent trial, he never expressed remorse or denied the crime. The jury convicted Butcher of all four murders and sentenced him to hang by the neck until dead.

One more surprise awaited. His will left his entire estate to the city with the proviso that they place a large monument over his grave. Most of the citizens were dead set against any memorial to this monster, but greed won the day, and the town commissioned and placed an obelisk over his body. The only word on the monument was his last name as required by his last will and testament. After laying the poor wife and children to rest elsewhere, everyone supposed the story was over. However, there have been many nocturnal sightings of his hung corpse swinging from a noose, and the ghost of Butcher with his razor would attack nighttime cemetery visitors.

Thrilled and chilled by our story, we tried to sleep. At some point, we woke with a start to screams and moans as counselors and senior campers attacked our campsite howling like banshees. We scattered shrieking in all directions thinking Butcher had come for us. They really overdid it, and it took until almost morning to round us all up again. Thinking death was imminent, we'd hidden really well.

The stream at Foundation Farm Camp

A counselor led kids from my cabin and a couple of others on a *stream stomp*. This entailed wading into a creek and walking downstream under bridges, roads and all the bends. I was wearing my tennis shoes and had stuck my socks into my pockets. Just as we approached a culvert under the road, I stomped onto a board with a long pro-

truding nail. The rusty underwater lance completely pen-
etrated the sole of my shoe, my left foot, and then came
out through the top of my tennis shoe. I howled and tried
to lift my foot out of the water. I was stuck to the bottom.
The board had other heavy debris on top of it. I yelled for
help and a counselor came to my rescue. He tried to pull
my leg up, thinking something had entrapped my foot, but
he stopped when I screamed. Feeling around, he found the
nail protruding through the top of my foot. He and another camper were able to free the board from the bottom
of the streambed, and it came out attached to my foot.

Lying on the grassy bank, I was the center of morbid
attention. Outside of statues in churches, none of us had
ever seen a crucifixion, even a partial one. It was obvious
I needed to return to camp, and I could not walk there myself. A counselor picked me up and carried me all the way
back to the nurse's cabin. The camp nurse quickly determined I required emergency room care, and someone
drove me to the local hospital. I really don't remember
how they got that nail out of my foot, but I am sure it involved painkiller drugs. They were concerned about teta-
nus, but the camp had insisted on our shots being up-to-
date and had records to prove it. They wrapped up my
foot, gave me antibiotics, and sent me back to camp. The
camp office called my grandmother, and she arrived soon
after my return. Sending me home with her was the ma-
jority verdict, but my abject begging carried the day, and
they grudgingly permitted me to remain a camper. There
was still another week of camp, and I was having such a
wonderful time!

O

O is for Officialdom
(Winter 2010)

December 27th, 2010. I was driving in the East African nation of Tanzania from Dar es Salaam to Bagamoyo, which is Swahili for "lay down your heart"—a reference to the town's historic and tragic role in the East African slave trade. My aim was some tourism among the famous ruins there and scouting out a place for my family to do a weekend retreat from our spartan accommodations in Mwandege Village. The drive was pretty nice once I'd cleared the clogged intersections of the capital city.

Everywhere you drive in Tanzania there are speed bumps put onto the road surface by localities to slow vehicle traffic. Often though, these bumps (or *sleeping policemen* as they're called in Malta) are completely unmarked, and they can launch your car airborne if you hit a large one without slowing. There are two varieties: the smaller four grouped close together for a corrugated effect, and the huge single lump. Often the smaller ones indicate the imminent arrival of the huge bump. You quickly learn that the smaller ones actually vibrate the car and passengers far less when you drive over them at regular speed rather than slowing down and crawling across them cautiously.

So I was stunned when, at 10:20 AM, about 10 kilometers outside Bagamoyo, a white Toyota Mark II sedan directly in front of me abruptly slammed on the brakes for a complete stop at a set of the small speed bumps. I hit my brakes and looked for a place to take evasive action, but with a truck coming along in the opposing lane, I was stuck. My car skidded forward and crunched the Mark II's right rear fender.

Unhurt myself and praying hard that everyone in the other car was okay as well, I pulled to the side of the road. The other vehicle just stopped right in the roadway. I got out, and the woman driving the Mark II followed suit. We established everyone was okay. Her name was Elizabeth, and she had young kids in the car—a boy and girl—neither in seat-belts. Then we assessed our vehicles. My car sustained some damage to bumper and lights, while her car's right rear bumper and quarter panel were somewhat damaged.

Several cars full of gawkers stopped. She persuaded one of the first to drive her kids into Bagamoyo and away from the scene. Her son was crying and seemed to object to his mom handing him over to the care of a stranger. I got the distinct impression she wanted to play this as if she had been driving alone in the car.

I assured her I had full collision insurance. She quickly suggested we handle this privately and not involve police or insurance companies. I was leery at the amount of damage and costs, but she suggested we turn around and return to Dar es Salaam, many miles away, to get an estimate. Not wanting to cancel my trip and feeling it would be better to submit it to insurance, I suggested waiting for the police report. About then, the police pulled up. Officer Hussein and a young traffic cop got out.

Officer Hussein asked if we planned to handle the accident privately, or if we wanted a police report. I again mentioned my insurance and suggested a police report was the correct procedure for submitting a claim. Hussein agreed and began drawing the scene of the accident. I made sure his rendition was accurate and included the two black skid marks from where I tried to stop my car.

About this time, Hussein received a call and explained a *mzungu* (white person) had her throat slashed and was found dead in a ditch as a result of a carjacking in Bagamoyo during the night. So, I figured the cops were going to be more than a little occupied, but I hoped they would take pains to help me, their surviving mzungu.

After they finished examining the scene, the lead officer instructed all of us to drive to the Bagamoyo Police Station. This turned out to be down a badly rutted dirt road at the south end of town. We pulled into a fenced yard at the station, and as I got out of my car, Officer Hussein asked me for my keys. He presented this as a mere formality and told me I'd receive them back as soon as I provided photocopy documentation of three things: vehicle registration, driver's license, and insurance cover letter. I questioned why the window sticker required by law was not sufficient proof of insurance since no one carries the cover letter in their car. But they insisted they needed the letter before they could release my car. I called my Zimbabwean friend, Vella, from Youth With A Mission— Mwandege, where we were living, and asked him to find the cover letter and fax or email it to me in Bagamoyo. I also asked him to call the insurance company to find out what I should be doing.

At this time, they led me to a room with a desk where Sgt. Paul would create the file and take the report. I answered his questions and provided the documentation I had, but he wanted photocopies. I had the registration and my driver's license, needing only to make the copies they wanted, so, owing to the lack of a copier at Police HQ, we drove a couple of kilometers into town to make copies.

In downtown Bagamoyo we parked at the NMB Bank where Elizabeth C. (the other party in the accident) was a manager. She went into her workplace, and Officer Hussein and I crossed the street to make copies of my license and registration. While we were doing this, Vella called and informed me that my insurance was so new the paperwork was still with the agent, and the office couldn't locate him. He also couldn't find a fax machine to send the cover letter, so he would have to go somewhere to either fax or scan and email the cover letter. I gave him Elizabeth's email to send it to.

Now the police had two-thirds of what they wanted, and Officer Hussein repeated over and over the three papers they needed. I kept telling him the copy of my insurance cover was on the way; he kept assuring me I could be on my way as soon as it arrived. At that moment I received a message from Vella and couldn't read it in the bright sunlight, so I told the policeman I would step into the bank to read it and reply. About two minutes later, I stepped back out and found the police, Elizabeth, and the police car that had driven me to town all gone!

I looked all over and asked around, but they were no longer in the vicinity. I was in a fix. I had no idea where I was or how to locate the police station, my car, and my belongings. The weather was steamy hot and my skin was burning. I wandered the road in the direction I guessed the police station might be. I asked for directions. After about 40 minutes I found an officer directing traffic at an intersection. He had a taxi take me back to the police station, at my expense.

When I got inside, my patience was gone. I asked them what Hussein was doing driving me away from the police

station and leaving me in town to wander lost. They explained he thought I would get myself some lunch while
we waited for the cover letter. It was now about one
o'clock. I called Vella. He said he had emailed the cover
letter scan, and Elizabeth should have received it.

She denied getting it. I suggested she return to the bank
and check her computer again, but she seemed reluctant.
Wanting to get my car and get out of their clutches, I
asked Vella to resend the email to my address. I took a cab
to get lunch and check my email at an internet café in
town.

After eating some chicken, I checked my email and was
able to print a perfect color scan of my insurance cover
letter. I had the taxi take me back to Police HQ so I could
present it and retrieve my car. When I arrived, Officer
Hussein and Sergeant Paul were both out, and I had to
wait for them. After an hour and a half, around 4:00, they
finally arrived with Elizabeth. The moment I handed over
the long-coveted insurance letter, both Hussein and Elizabeth pronounced it a fake and a forgery—as if they'd
scripted their response in advance. I instantly realized this
was a scam for the big dollars they were trying to wring
from me. The last thing any of them wanted was for me
to submit the claim to insurance. They planned to make it
impossible for me to leave Bagamoyo without paying everyone off.

I completely lost my temper at this point. Working all
day to get a paper, followed by an accusation of forgery
was too much! I'd acted in honesty and good faith and dis-

covered I had played the fool. I started yelling and demanding that if they believed I committed a crime they
must charge and arrest me. I was standing where I could
see their jail cell--a small room with a bucket for a toilet
and a barred door. There were four shirtless sweating men
inside, and they looked miserable. The police appeared
shocked at my response and refused to arrest me. They
said they couldn't arrest me and that I should just go to a
hotel. I refused to leave without my car; I told them I'd
provided 100% of what they asked for, and they were
breaking their promise.

They responded with a repetition of doubt about the
legitimacy of my cover letter and now demanded someone
drive several hours to bring the original cover letter! I responded if I had faked it, then I'd committed a crime, and
they must jail me. This went on and on, around and
around, louder and louder. One fat cop screamed at me
and made me sit on the cement floor right outside the cell.
I continued demanding they lock me up and began to film
a bit with my video camera, which led the fat cop to
scream to turn it off and put it away. It was clear they
didn't feel their treatment of me would withstand scru-
tiny. I made friends with the four prisoners behind bars
and slipped one some shillings. No one fed inmates unless
relatives brought food. His family was in far-off Arusha,
so he was starving.

Around dinnertime, they told me the Prosecutor was
outside waiting to speak with me. I objected to talking to
a prosecutor without charges or a lawyer. They hastened
to assure me that, as second in command, the Prosecutor

was acting as Police Chief at the moment, the Station Chief being out of town. I headed outside in the dusk to talk with him and ask him for my car keys. He said giving me my keys would be impossible until the court heard my case. I was livid! Not only was this the first mention of a court case in the entire day-long ordeal, but this new information made a complete lie of the entire procedure (as explained ad nauseam by Hussein) thus far. The papers I had worked all day to provide now seemed to be a colossal waste of time. I renewed my demands for arrest. He told me they would have my court case heard at 7:00 the following morning. He instructed me to go to a hotel. I refused, stating, "I'm staying at the jail, either inside or outside the cell." Then I stomped back to my seat on the floor.

At 7:00 it was dark and all the policemen began to leave for the night. Eventually only two young officers, the prisoners, and two women who had also been sitting on the floor since I'd returned after lunch remained. One woman had been screaming at the cops for some time before I had begun my tirade. I didn't have a clue what they were in for. (I later found police had accused the screamer of carjacking and murdering the white man, even though she'd been in another town at the time. Since they had no one else in custody for the crime, they were keeping her even though they knew it was a false accusation.)

One of the two young policemen was actually quite nice. The second never said a word. Emmanuel, the nice cop, told me what the police were doing to me was wrong: they should give me the keys because I'd done everything they asked, and they had no reason or right to keep me or my car. He admitted their motive was greed, and they were waiting for a bribe. He seemed very ashamed of his bosses, but he was low man on the totem pole and had no power. He begged me to allow him to call a taxi to take me to a guesthouse. He was so concerned for me and was horrified at the thought of me spending the night there outside the cell door where I'd parked myself. His kind concern weakened my resolve, and I gave in to his pleadings. I finally left the police station about 8:30 pm—almost 10 hours after arriving.

I spent the night at a cheap guesthouse with no air conditioning. I was so hot I couldn't sleep. I opened all the windows in my room to try to catch a breeze; the night watchman came by and closed them all. He was worried about thieves reaching in through the windows. I was more worried about suffocation. Besides, I was in better with the criminal element of Bagamoyo than law enforcement. Finally I left the room and found a boy who worked at the guesthouse. He came in and reopened all my windows, but it was still stifling, so he moved me to a corner room where two walls had windows. That was an improvement, but I still didn't get much sleep.

DEC 28, DAY TWO:

In the morning I had to call my taxi driver at 6:30 in order to get to the Police HQ in time for the promised 7:00 court session, so I missed the breakfast that was included with my room. When I arrived, only Emmanuel was on duty, and he said they wouldn't be coming in for another hour. I eventually understood there would be no court that day, and nothing had changed from the day before. I then stomped out for a walk along the nearby beach. I ended up at the ruins of a Portuguese fort and some German Custom House ruins. Behind these I found a restaurant, The Smoke House, which served breakfast burritos! I ordered one and met the proprietress, Teddy, who was Tanzanian and was married to a Texan. When she heard my story, she filled me in on her family's adventures with local police corruption and confirmed all I had been guessing. She insisted on helping me. We drove out to her house, and I got to know her husband while she called the police chief who was out of town and unaware of what had transpired. He promised to call the station and try to resolve things. So, the three of us decided the most important thing to do was to get my car out of that police yard. We jumped into their car and drove over to Police HQ.

Along the way, Teddy's husband shared his view that if I had to pay a few hundred dollars to the woman, it would be far cheaper than going through the courts and getting every other corrupt official's hand in my pocket. If the two drivers settle, then there is no case, and they must release the vehicle. We found Elizabeth at the Police Station and Teddy spoke with her about what a deal would take. She still wanted to get an estimate from a particular body shop in Dar es Salaam, so to get things moving we agreed to go with her to get it. Elizabeth wanted to leave my car in impound, but I insisted we bring it along. Elizabeth was so afraid I'd take my car and flee, she made Teddy post a personal bond of two million shillings ($1300 dollars) with the police as *bail* for me and the car. She also had a friend drive my car and Teddy the 45 miles to Dar es Salaam, while she made me ride with her in her car. I had to be pleasant since the whole trip was in hope of finding a reasonable solution acceptable to all. I phoned Vella, who'd already decided I was in way too deep and needed help, and was already on his way with a Tanzanian businessman friend, Fortune. I'd met Fortune while shopping for the Toyota Corolla three months earlier. We all agreed to meet up at Kevin's Chinese Auto Service Center. I was so relieved to have some local allies on their way.

Before we could leave Bagamoyo, Elizabeth drove to her bank where she said she needed to say goodbye. After cooking in the parked car for 25 minutes, I went into the bank to find her. She was engaged in forming a queue out of the mob waiting to talk to the single teller. I told her we had to go and we needed to be respectful of Teddy's time. (After all, Teddy had no reason to be along at all except Elizabeth had insisted upon it, apparently afraid a prominent restaurant owner would also flee to deprive her of her repair money.) She begged for a "few more minutes" to help in the bank. I went out to update Teddy and the driver. After another ten minutes I again went in looking for her. I couldn't see her anywhere, so I opened the door to her office. Elizabeth was shoveling food into her face and looked up like the cat that swallowed the canary. Her excuse for eating in her air-conditioned office while we baked? "I am hungry and can't drive while I eat." I offered to drive her car while she fed herself, and so, after some more queue repair on her way out, we at last were off for

Dar es Salaam. But not until we gassed up her car and she extorted $20 from me to pay for the fuel. This didn't bode well for the success of the trip. She was definitely not after a win-win solution.

On the way to the body shop, Elizabeth told me to expect to pay her two million Tanzanian Schillings (TS) for the repairs. I replied it was premature for her to set an amount before the appraiser had given his estimate, but she was adamant. Hoping she was wrong and feeling queasy that the body shop was in cahoots, I kept to myself that I would turn it in to the insurance company if the amount was so out-of-bounds. She also explained I must pay her the entire estimate and she would pay for the repairs, unless they overran the estimate, in which case I'd have to cover the additional amount as well. We detoured to pick up her father and thereby missed picking up Vella and Fortune. I called Vella and directed him to the shop, which we reached at long last.

Elizabeth had been on the phone with this garage since the accident, and my suspicion they'd worked out a deal grew. Sure enough, they quickly produced a ridiculous estimate for 3.2 million TS. Vella told her in this case we would need to let my insurance handle things. Elizabeth started yelling like a lunatic. She called Vella a "bush lawyer" and refused to speak with him again. She called me a liar for not instantly handing over "her money." She told me "You will pay for this!" She then placed a call to her driver, who then sped away from the garage in my car—supposedly returning it to the Bagamoyo police impound.

We noticed it had a flat tire and had to beg Elizabeth to call her driver and insist he change it.

Vella, Fortune, Teddy and I decided there was nothing left to do but head back north to Bagamoyo. At this point Elizabeth actually grabbed Teddy and forced her to drive with her as surety—though we couldn't figure this as she had possession of my car as well. I refused to ride back with Elizabeth since she was abusing me loudly with her every utterance—yet still insisting I ride *hostage* with her. I began to doubt her sanity. Vella, Fortune and I made the hour return trek to Bagamoyo Police HQ and arrived to find neither my car nor Elizabeth's had returned. Elizabeth had called the police and accused me of stealing my own car from her! Since she and my car were both AWOL, it was pretty clear I didn't have it. We called Teddy and learned they were all at the bank. It took some doing, but finally we were all back where we'd been that morning. Only now, the mood was ugly.

We decided it was top priority to get Teddy off the hook and disconnected from this messy morass. We convinced the police to give Teddy her signed bond back, as they had the car (and me!). Fortune called a friend in government and got a person on the police force who would secretly work for our interests. We had a mole! Elizabeth went into overdrive trying to foul everything. She started meeting with every official she could find—this behavior continued until long after midnight! Her plan now was to deny me a court date entirely and tie up my car until I paid her the riches she coveted. Vella, Fortune and I checked into a brand new guesthouse Teddy had shown us as we drove her home. As soon as I paid and we were in our rooms, Fortune explained he must to go back into town to start meeting with officials to reach a satisfactory conclusion before court the next morning. We offered to go with him, but he believed our *foreign* presence would greatly complicate his task. Apparently Vella, the Zimbabwean "bush lawyer" had angered the authorities with his logical arguments and for coming between them and their cash cow: me. As the supposedly rich *mzungu*, my involvement snarled everything. Fortune hoped to use diplomacy to find out what was really going on and who wanted what. Abashed, we watched him drive off alone into the vipers' nest.

Fortune returned twice, but each time received a call and had to rush out again for more meetings. He informed us Elizabeth was meeting with all the same officials and telling incredible lies about us. Her goal was clearly to prevent a court date at any cost and to force me to pay her to get my car back. Fortune was still at it when Vella and I went to bed at 11:00.

DEC 29, DAY THREE:

On this morning, I woke up and realized we had to really hurry to get the breakfast included with our rooms and get over to the police station and thence to court. Fortune was exhausted. He had been at his politicking most of the night. Over breakfast he explained that for a *tip* of around $50 to two officials, the prosecutor and the judge, I would get my day in court that morning. The alternative was that court would never happen, and my car would stay in Bagamoyo Police custody until Elizabeth received her payoff. Since there would be no police report issued without a court judgment, my insurance company would not be paying for the damages to either car. It was clear the wheels of justice in Bagamoyo were in serious need of some grease. If I paid the requested bribes, for that was what they were of course, then the officials and Fortune would agree on a verdict in advance of court. I would say, "Yes," to everything in a prepared statement they would read. They would reach a verdict of guilty and the sentence would be a nominal fine. Then I'd pay the fine, receive a receipt, and get my car keys from the police. I would have a report for the insurance company, and they would take over dealing with Elizabeth. By this point, the arrangement sounded like a great deal, and I took it.

Fortune went off to grease palms, and Vella and I waited at the police station. When Fortune returned, we all drove over to the courthouse. It was basically a roof over an open gallery with benches already filling up with people. We took our seats and waited while we watched the clerk and bailiff move around huge stacks of files at the front tables. We could see the Judge's chambers behind them. It was hot and all the doors were open. I was pleased to see Elizabeth seemed to have slept in and missed her day in court.

Unfortunately, just after the announcement stating court was about to begin, but before the judge appeared, Elizabeth pulled up in a cab and made a beeline for the back door to the Judge's chambers. I was astonished something so obviously unjust and prejudicial occurred in broad daylight and in full view of over 200 people. I told

Fortune she was upsetting the applecart, but he told me to relax, there was nothing she could do now to alter the pre-arranged outcome of my case.

After another thirty minutes, during which the only excitement was the catching of a small green snake on the road outside the courtroom, which caused at least a third of those in court to run over and join the shouting, snake-catching mob, they finally called my case. To my surprise, the bailiff instructed me to go outside and around the back of the court and enter the judge's private chambers. Fortune went with me while my "bush lawyer" had to wait outside. Inside were the prosecutor and the judge, who was sitting at his desk. The windows were open for any stray breeze, yet the office was an oven. Some citizens came over to watch through the window, and the bailiff chased them off. I complied when they asked me to present the same ID and documents the police had already possessed for two days. Then Elizabeth came huffing in and plopped her ample bottom down on the only other chair. She was glaring, but not daring to say anything. I think it was beginning to occur to her something had happened and things were not going her way.

A court officer from the next room entered and found a place to stand in the now crowded chamber. Someone handed him a page of charges to read. As he read, he would pause after each sentence and the prosecutor indicated I should say "yes" or "no" in answer to each. This was the first time I had heard the charge against me, which was: "Causing damages through careless driving." He went on to read the "Particulars of the Offense," which were as follows:

[sic] "That BRIAN PATRICK HOGAN charged the 27th day of December, 2010 at about 10:20 hours at Zinga Road, within Bagamoyo District, Coast region being driver and Incharge of Motor Vehicle with Registration No. T 579 ALF Make Toyota Corolla Saloon, did drive the said Motor Vehicle on the Public Road carelessly without care to other Road users to wit you knocked Motor Vehicle with Registration N. T 332 BDW make Toyota Mark II Saloon which was driving the same direction as results you caused damages to both Motor Vehicles."

As agreed, I said, "Yes," to everything, even when they pulled out the drawing of the accident scene. It was obvious Officer Hussein had redrawn it the night before. The new drawing eliminated the skid marks, which had featured prominently in his original. Elizabeth had paid well to bury evidence casting her in a bad light. The new drawing gave no indication that she had stopped, or I had attempted to brake to avoid hitting her. I was tempted to protest for the record, but realized it would only complicate and delay things that were set to go my way regardless of the evidence. If she had produced a box of severed heads from my killing spree, all I had to do was admit it and receive a small fine. Everything was scripted. Therefore, asked if the drawing was accurate, I replied, "Yes."

Then the judge looked at me and said, "Now is the time for mitigation." It didn't seem like the yes or no questions Fortune had prepared me for in rehearsal, so I just stood there silently facing him. Everyone looked at me in clear expectation of speech. I had nothing. Finally the judge decided to elucidate.

"This is when you plead for the mercy of the court."

"Oh, okay. Ummm . . . this is my first time in a court-room. I am a good person who doesn't break laws. I am very sorry for any car knocking that may have occurred in your district. I promise if you let me go I will never return to the Bagamoyo area or knock any other cars here."

"You should come back to our city. There are many wonderful things to see here."

"No, I will never return. I have seen enough."

A long, silent and uncomfortable pause in the proceedings ensued until the judge said, "Now is the time of sentencing." I waited with bated breath.

"You are found guilty of the charge and must either pay the fine of 30,000 Tanzanian Schillings ($20 US dollars) or be sentenced to two years in prison."

I had to really struggle to not burst out in laughter. What a tough decision! Could I have some time to think it over?

"I'll pay the fine, Your Honor."

Immediately, everyone except the judge stood, and we all filed out. Elizabeth stalked out fuming. Fortune guided me over to a counter where I gave a clerk the cash and, after waiting about 25 minutes on the street outside, I received a handwritten receipt. It was over.

We drove back to the police station in Fortune's car and presented my receipt to the policewoman, who Fortune now quietly revealed to be his mole. She gave me my car keys and we went out to find that while in police custody the tire had again gone flat and the front passenger door handle had been broken. We jacked up the car and waited while Fortune drove the tire off for repair. While waiting, the policewoman asked me for money for her services. At the end of all patience with this attitude that all my money is actually theirs and only waiting for transfer to Tanzanians, I told her I was broke from paying fines and bribes and I could not give her anything. Awkward. Finally, the tire arrived and the car was again roadworthy. I can't describe how good it felt to pull out of the police yard after three days of insanity.

Fortune was extremely overdue at home and, after I gassed up his car, he took off at once toward Dar es Salaam. Vella and I took my car to a service station to have the spare tire repaired. Our plan was to take a smaller coastal road back south so the entire trip would not be devoid of tourism. I had seen there were ruins of a town on the coast where Henry Morton Stanley and other famous explorers landed before pushing into the dark interior of Africa. There was also a Crocodile Farm the GPS pointed out.

However before we even set out, Fortune called to say his internet modem was still in Vella's pocket. Fortune was about 10 kilometers south on the main road, so Vella had to divert our course to return the modem. Our route toward the scenic coastal road brought us uncomfortably close to the hated police station. But our decision to take this route turned out to be worthwhile. Vella and I enjoyed our drive. The ruins and the crocs provided an interesting diversion from our surreal experiences in Bagamoyo. We stopped at my favorite Lebanese place where I treated for dinner. When we finally pulled into

YWAM Mwandege and reunited with Louise, my son Peter, and the rest of the Birth Attendant School outreach team, a cheer went up. My return was the answer to many prayers.

I arranged to have the insurance adjuster view the car and approve the repairs and then took Peter on safari for three days to give the garage a chance to fix my car. When we returned, they had not even started with the repairs because they were waiting for a letter from my insurance company. I got this sorted out and repairs commenced. I noticed Elizabeth's Toyota Mark II was at the same body shop.

A couple of days before I collected my vehicle, I heard from Elizabeth one last time. She called my mobile phone and sweetly asked how I was doing. I answered, "Fine," and waited.

She said, "I called to ask how you are doing."

"I told you, fine." . . . silence . . .

Me: "I am wondering the reason for your call."

Her: "You are wondering the reason for my call?"

Me: "Yes, I am wondering why you called me."

Her: "You are wondering why I called you?"

Me: "Yes."

Her: "To ask how you are doing."

Me: "Oh. Fine." Long silence. "Is there anything else?"

Her: "Oh, I had a question."

Me: "Yes?"

Her: "My car is not finished, and I have nothing to drive. It is quite a hardship."

Me: "Me too. I rented a car."

Her: "Would you rent me a car?"

Me: "No."

Her: "But you knocked my car and your insurance company says you don't have coverage for a rental car so my lawyer said I should ask you."

Me: "You should talk to the insurance company and ask for whatever you need. It is between you and them. There is nothing for you to talk to me about. We went to court. Remember? You obtained a judgment, and it went to the insurance company. You need to take it up with them."

Her: "But they won't . . . "

Me: "Then have your lawyer get them to provide one. Have a nice day. Good bye." And I hung up the phone.

Epilogue:

It took two weeks to get my car back from the shop and many calls to the insurance company to get the letter the shop needed in original (they only had a fax) to release my car, but I finally picked it up on Monday, January 17 (the day before my 49th birthday).

It looked great.

P

P is for Poison

(1982)

... they will take snakes in their hands, they will drink poison and not be hurt ...

—Jesus in Mark 16:18 (MSG)

Vizzini: *(sniffs vial) "I smell nothing."*

Man in Black: *"What you do not smell is called Iocane powder. It is odorless, tasteless, dissolves instantly in liquid, and is among the more deadly poisons known to man."*

—The Princess Bride

A sophomore studying at California Polytechnic State University in San Luis Obispo, I was taking classes for a degree in Natural Resource Management. This was just prior to switching to an English major the next quarter, brought on by my call to missions. One of my more taxing courses was Plant Taxonomy. The course consisted of two parts—a rigorous lecture and a lab section. For lecture I sat under Professor Riggins, a rather severe woman whose research obsession was *Lupinus*, commonly known as lupine, a genus of flowering plants in the legume family. I found her manner rather intimidating and her exams near impossible. My grades in her part of the class were averaging D–, and my only hope was snagging an A in the lab section to balance this.

Dr. David Keil, one of my favorite professors at Cal Poly, oversaw the botany lab. This tall academic was an engaging teacher who managed to make Plant Taxonomy fun. We went on field trips to identify plants in places from around the campus, to the Oceano dunes, and out to the salt marshes of Morro Bay. Even the exams in his lab were an adventure.

Having flunked my final in Dr. Riggins' lecture hall, I came into my lab final aware quite a lot was riding on my performance. Upon entering the lab, I noticed the long black tables covered with an assortment of cardboard boxes. As we entered, the Prof told us to take our seats and avoid touching anything on the tables. Dr. Keil explained the exam. We were to move from station to station, lift the box in front of us and identify the plant found underneath. We were only allowed our large text—a key to California plants, and a pen and paper. We were to note the number of the box and after keying out its contents, write the scientific name of the plant in front of us.

Dr. Keil set the timer, and the exam was underway. I enjoyed flipping through the book chasing down the plant from feature to feature. "Monocot or Dicot?" Dicot. So turn to the page indicated: "Are the leaf blades pinnately veined or parallel-veined?" Choosing the former led to "Leaves and stems—differentiated or not?", "Plants woody or herbaceous?" and so on. The branching answers to each question led to new pages and new questions and eventually to the exact species. Depending upon which feature of the plant one chose to start with, there were a variety of paths through the key that would lead to the final correct identification. I was making very good time and felt quite confident about my discoveries. I certainly had a chance of pulling an overall C in Plant Taxonomy.

As I lifted the box at my fourth station, I saw a stalked plant resembling oversized celery with purple blotches. This was intriguing. I'd never seen it before. I picked an initial feature and plunged in. About seven dichotomous branches into my search for the plant's identity, the key asked this question: "Is the taste reminiscent of celery?" It was a straight yes or no question. I couldn't think of any way of arriving at the answer short of actually having a small nibble. Mindful of the fact there were many students coming along after me, I didn't want to be a glutton. I stripped off a small side stalk and took a bite. I chewed it carefully, analyzing the taste, and determined it was unremarkable, but certainly not at all like celery. Having decided the answer was *no*, I quickly flipped to the page indicated by that answer. Plunging ahead and mindful of the exam time constraints, I reached my answer in another four steps.

Cicuta douglasii—Western Water Hemlock.

Crud! I'd just eaten what Athens used to execute Socrates! Why would the book ask me to taste anything for which one of the possible answers was a poisonous plant?

"The main distinguishable characteristic of Western Water Hemlock is its toxicity. Cicutoxin is the toxin produced by the water hemlock, **making it the most poisonous plant in North America.**" (Wikipedia)

North America's most toxic plant

I walked up to the front desk where Dr. Keil was overseeing the exam.

"Excuse me! Dr. Keil? I've just eaten a small bit of the specimen at station 12."

Opening a folder to glance briefly at his answer key, he whispered, "Number 12 is hemlock. Whatever possessed you to eat it?"

"I know what it is: Western Water Hemlock." I was still keen to get credit for the answer. "I finished keying it out before I came to tell you. I only ate some because the book asked about the taste."

"That's ridiculous! The plant key would never suggest a taste test in anything that could branch to a poisonous species."

"I would've thought the same and yet, it does." I opened my key and proceeded to show him the page where it asked about the taste. Dr. Keil appeared shocked such a thing had made it past the editors. He explained Western Water Hemlock contained a powerful and dangerous alkaloid poison. He had his student assistant take over proctoring the final exam and asked me to accompany him to his office. I was reluctant because the lost exam time would have a negative impact on my grade. He assured he'd give me an opportunity to make it up.

As soon as we reached his office, Dr. Keil called the Poison Information Service. A conversation ensued of which I only heard his half. At one point he relayed a question to me about my weight. I told him I was about 200 pounds. After he relayed this, there was a pause. Dr. Keil chuckled, thanked the person on the other end and hung up the phone.

He seemed quite relieved as he told me, "Well, you're in the clear. The amount of hemlock you consumed was not enough to endanger you. At your size you'd need to graze on hemlock to get enough to poison you." We returned to the classroom, and I picked up my exam where I'd left off. When the buzzer sounded and all tests handed in, Dr. Keil stayed on while I completed my exam.

I aced the final. My combined grade in Plant Taxonomy was a solid C.

Postscript: In researching this story I learned the information they gave us about the quantity at which hemlock becomes a danger to humans was rather under-stated. Even three ounces would have been enough to do me in.

Western Water Hemlock contains a toxin which " . . . is an unsaturated alcohol that has a major impact on the central nervous system of animals. Early symptoms of cicutoxin poisoning include excessive salivation, frothing at the mouth, nervousness, and incoordination." (This describes my standard reaction to final exams.) "These symptoms can turn into tremors, muscular weakness, seizures and respiratory failure. Very small amounts of green materials of Western Water Hemlock, about .1% of a person's body weight (< 3 ounces in my case) can even lead to death . . . . Death can occur within fifteen minutes of ingesting this toxin." (Wikipedia)

Sixteen years later I was sharing our Mongolia story in a Perspectives class at Grace Church in San Luis Obispo. One of the students approached me during the break. It was Dr. David Keil! The first thing he did was to ask me if I remembered eating hemlock during his exam. Apparently my inadvertent application of the Socratic method in his final had made me memorable among the thousands of students that had passed through his classes over the decades. He and his wife Kathy are disciples of Jesus and were excitedly absorbing everything they could about God's purposes among the nations. We had a wonderful time catching up, and later I shared the story of the hemlock with the class. David and Kathy soon became our friends and supporters.

Q

Q is for Quackery
(Fall 2000)

Marcus the Physician called yesterday on the marble Zeus.

Through marble and through Zeus, the funeral is today.

—Nicarchus, in the *Greek Anthology*

It had been a rough night. I tossed and turned until the wee hours of the morning. Suddenly sharp pains in my guts and nausea drove me out of bed and into the tiny toilet room of the Mongolian apartment. As I sat there, desperate for whatever was causing my problem to empty out from one end or the other, I realized I could have hardly picked a worse time or place to fall ill.

It was our penultimate night in Mongolia after a short two-week visit. In two days my family and I would be flying back across the Pacific to our home in Northern California. It had been hard enough to tear ourselves away to make this trip to revisit the land where God had done so much through and for our family. We had to get the girls excused from school, and ask teammates to cover our responsibilities in the two schools we were running: a YWAM *Frontier Mission Discipleship Training School* and a Perspectives course. When our Mongolian disciples in Erdenet had contacted us and invited us to return to teach church planting in their School of Frontier Mission, everyone had agreed it was time to revisit Mongolia as a family. Since our departure in 1996, I'd made two teaching trips but Louise and the children had never returned. Four years before, our youngest, Peter Magnus, had left Mongolia in his mother's womb.

We'd had a marvelous visit. The training went well. During my time with the school, I'd managed to pass the training baton on to a disciple, Bayaraa, who had both the teaching gift and church planting experience. She'd worked with our team from 1993 to 1996 to plant the Church of Erdenet. Having made this transfer, I'd never need to teach church planting in Mongolia again. We spent all our free time catching up with dear Mongolian friends and enjoying the hospitality in which this people excel. The day before my nocturnal attack, we'd spent time touring the church's property outside of town. Our former disciples showed us greenhouses full of vegetables being grown to feed the poor, a soup kitchen serving the city's street children, and a number of other mercy ministries utilizing that property. At one point I was told a donated cow was about to be killed and butchered. Three young volunteers from the church, all city boys, were taking on this task. There is a kind of national conceit that every Mongolian is born with the knowledge of all necessary animal husbandry skills. I had seen evidence of the fanciful nature of this belief in prior experiences with urban Mongolians, particularly teens. I eagerly went over to watch what promised to be quite a show.

There were already other observers waiting near the sacrificial victim. I was surprised to see one of them looked to be an American. Introducing myself, I discovered he was a short-term medical missionary who happened to be passing through Erdenet. Dr. Bob from Arkansas was a genial and personable fellow, and we fell into easy camaraderie without delay. Since no one else spoke English, we could talk freely without fear of giving offense. I shared with Dr. Bob my guess that our first-time butchers would put on a performance worthy of *The Three Stooges*.

The boys began by winding rope around the cow's legs in an attempt to immobilize it. Then one of them, carrying an axe, boldly walked up to the front end and cracked the cow with a mighty blow with the blunt end right between its horns. It didn't even break the skin. The surprised animal made a loud and angry protestation, and the boy whacked it again. The other two pulled mightily on the rope in an attempt to yank the cow's legs out from under it. This effort did not immediately bear fruit, and the yanking continued to the tune of bovine basso profundo vocalizations that, had they been human would have made a sailor blush. Once the cow was finally lying on its side bellowing and eyes rolling horribly, one of the rope pullers produced a massive butcher knife and plunged it up to the handle into the cow's chest. Some blood spurted out and the cow's panic seemed to increase, but beyond this there was no discernible difference noted. Our Mongol Jack the Ripper tried two additional stabs in the same vicinity to no avail.

I asked Dr. Bob, "Can this patient be saved?" He replied, "In a good trauma unit? Without a doubt." We chuckled, not because we were callous. It was either laugh or cry. The butchers were growing increasingly panicked by the cow's stubborn refusal to become meat. After five minutes of increasingly frantic attempts, the knife wielder got lucky. Holding the knife deep into the wound he levered it in every direction possible until it nicked something vital. With a final shudder their victim finally perished. I never had the opportunity to taste the meat, but both Bob and I imagined the sharp tang of adrenaline would marinate it. We bonded over the shared horror we'd witnessed and ended up sharing dinner together, though neither of us ordered beef.

So, sitting in the toilet room way too early on the morning of October 18th, 2000, with an ache deep in my guts, I assumed it must have been something I ate. This is not at all uncommon in Mongolia, after all. Dawn seemed to take an eternity, but when Louise awoke and I filled her in, she concurred it was probably food poisoning. Louise, in her inimitable compassion-free manner urged me, "Just throw up, you'll feel better." The only concern was that I might not be well enough to travel in time for our flight home. Louise decided to call Dr. Bob and see if he could make a house call before he left Erdenet. When my new

friend arrived, he asked a bunch of questions before per-
forming a simple test. He pushed two fingers deep into the
right side of my belly. He asked me if it hurt. "Not really,"
I replied. "What about now?" Dr. Bob asked and suddenly
withdrew his fingers. Aaaaaaaaaaaaaaaah!" was my response. Without a trace of his habitual smile he revealed
his diagnosis. Appendicitis.

It was imperative I get somewhere an emergency appendectomy could be performed. The hospital in Erdenet
had a fairly grim reputation, and we rejected that out of
hand. Louise and Dr. Bob decided he should call Blue Sky
Aviation, the Mongolian branch of MAF (Missionary
Aviation Fellowship), and see if they could send a plane up
to Erdenet for an evacuation to Ulaanbaatar and better
hospitals.

What followed was a jouncing ride in an overcrowded
Russian 69 (jeep) with poor shocks on mostly dirt roads
that caused my painfully inflamed middle untold agonies.
Luckily, it wasn't very long before we were eleven miles
from city limits at Erdenet's abandoned airport. It soon began to snow and we all went upstairs into the empty control tower to watch for the plane's arrival. Vandals (or
former air traffic controllers) had removed all of the elec-
tronics, and the room was a shambles. The pain in my side
was becoming particularly intense and everyone understood things needed to move quickly. However, until the
plane arrived, all we could do was wait while the snow de-
creased visibility. After about an hour, we spied a motorcycle coming out of the curtain of blowing snow down the
runway toward us. We went downstairs to greet the rider,

and as he pulled off the scarf wrapped around his head, we saw our disciple, Nyamlaoweg. He had come bearing bad news. The Mongolian aviation authorities had denied MAF permission to make the flight, citing the snowstorm and the unknown runway conditions. (We knew. We'd seen the runway, cracked and with grasses sprouting through.) It was official—I was trapped in Erdenet. There was no way I'd survive the overnight railway trip to the capital city.

It was a somber and dispirited group that piled back into the Jeep for the trip back into town. On the way, they discussed where to take me. I participated between sessions of moaning. I vehemently vetoed the hospital, and made it clear my best option would be a small Russian clinic I knew. I'd discovered this *Prophylacticura* five years before when a Russian friend set up a massage for me there. I'd never returned, finding the massage far too medical and too little relaxing. But I knew they provided whatever medical treatment the Russian residents of Erdenet required. I figured they must have an operating theater and a surgeon. Through teeth clenched by pain, I managed to direct the driver to this almost hidden mini-hospital.

As soon as we entered the brick building, the very imposing Russian receptionist lady made it clear we were the wrong nationality to receive care there. Dr. Bob got very close to her face and said one word very loudly, careful to enunciate each syllable: "AP-PEN-DIX." She backed down immediately and scurried to find the doctor. My memories of the next half hour are near nonexistent. I remember strangers' hands stripping me and helping me onto a wheeled table. I assume they performed a number of other indignities upon me because I was in surgery an hour and

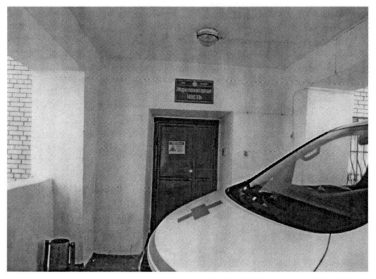

Entrance to Russian Clinic in Erdenet, Mongolia

a half after we walked in.

When I came to, I met my Russian surgeon and was surprised to hear him explain in English he had removed a leaking appendix from me and that I was very lucky I'd come in when I had. I'd been in much danger, but he assured me his surgical skill had made that danger a thing of the past. He apologized for the huge incision, and told me that although he was a laparoscopic specialist, this benighted provincial clinic was not equipped for laparoscopy. Still a bit groggy, I managed to shake his hand and thank him. He left and sent in Louise, who was relieved to see me looking so much better. Dr. Bob had caught the evening train and was on his way to Ulaanbaatar. Louise and I talked for a while and thanked God together after which she left to allow me to sleep some more.

Over the following day I received visits from Louise and the children, every missionary we knew in the city, and many of our Mongolian friends. The people running the hospital were not accustomed to Mongolians coming in as their usual clientele tended to have few Mongolian friends. After initially attempting to discourage our Mongolian friends from visiting, they seemed to decide an American patient was an exceptional case. Of course, I also received visits from doctors and nurses and experienced what seemed like excellent care. The nurse made it quite clear that my leaving in four days, as planned, was now an impossibility. Louise and I came to the very difficult conclusion she and the children would need to go home without me. The girls needed to get back to school and Louise needed to relieve those carrying our responsibilities at home. I would have to make my way home when they released me and when I was fit to travel.

So it was Louise and my children who made a final visit to my small stark and boring hospital room to say goodbye for what we thought would be about a week. I managed to stand up to give my wife a final hug. As we parted, I could feel my hospital gown clinging to my stomach in a moist and disgusting manner. I looked down and Louise followed my gaze. We were both shocked to see a large wet brown spreading stain over the site of my incision. A foul odor wafted up from it as well. Louise and the kids were going to miss their train if they didn't leave, so she said on the way out she'd send the nurse to check my wound and bring me a fresh gown. I lay back down and everyone gave me a last kiss before heading to the waiting taxi.

When the nurse came in, she took one look at my weeping wound and left immediately. A few minutes later my surgeon came in and examined me. Even though he struggled for some of the words in English it was very clear he was quite concerned over what I understood to be an opportunistic postoperative infection: concerned enough to tell me I needed to go back under the knife. I pleaded with him to try other less invasive procedures first. He insisted the only thing to do was to go back in and clean me out. The discussion was over.

Meanwhile, Louise and our children were making the long and laborious journey back to our home in McKinleyville, California. As soon as she could catch her breath, Louise composed and sent out a letter asking for prayer (following up an earlier brief emailed plea).

How can I begin? The kids and I returned from Mongolia a week ago. Unfortunately we had to leave Brian behind in a Russian hospital, in Erdenet, recovering from an emergency appendectomy. (Is there any other kind?)

It all started on the morning of Oct. 18. All six of us were in Erdenet for the first time since we left four years ago. Brian taught in the Mongolia Mission Center, at the beginning of the week. He woke early in the morning with severe stomach pains. My initial thought was that he had just eaten something bad, which is common in Mongolia. I told him, "Just throw up and you'll feel better." How's that for compassion? By mid-morning I suggested that we call the American doctor who just "happened" to be visiting Erdenet. Dr. Bob came and poked and asked questions for an hour. He then said that he was 85% sure that it was appendicitis.

Now we had to consider our options. We decided the best thing would be to get Brian to Ulaanbaatar for surgery. However, God had other plans. Missionary Aviation Fellowship (MAF) said they could send an eight-seat plane to pick up all six of us and Dr. Bob. With a light snow blowing, we loaded ten people and our luggage into a small jeep and headed out to the air field. After an 18 km. bumpy ride we arrived at the abandoned airport. The word airport is a bit grandiose for an unheated, unfurnished building in middle of the steppe. We waited for a half an hour while the kids played ping-pong on the only piece of furniture in the place. Then a friend from church rode up on his motorcycle to say that the plane was not coming; MAF was denied permission to fly to Erdenet. We piled back into the jeep for the ride back to town. Through it all Brian remained remarkably patient, even though his gut was on fire. He commented that he'd always longed to visit the airport in Erdenet.

We drove straight to the Russian hospital and dropped off Bob and Brian. That was about 5:30 in the evening and Brian was in surgery by 7 PM. The Russian doctor who did the surgery told us the next day the appendix enlarged three to four times its normal size and had begun to leak. Thank you, God, Dr. Bob was there to diagnose the problem.

Four days later, the kids and I took the overnight train to the capital city to catch our flight home. It was hard to leave Brian behind, especially since we discovered his wound was infected. When I asked Brian if he still wanted me to go he said he would feel better knowing we were safe at home. On Monday *they had to reopen the incision and clean out the infection. My informants tell me it went well. At this moment we don't know when he will be home or even when he will leave the hospital.*

Thank you to those of you who already heard and have been praying. Please continue to pray for Brian. He still has a long journey ahead of him, filled with planes, trains, and automobiles. Please feel free to phone, e-mail or write for an update. Blessings! Louise, for the Hogans

I awoke from this second surgery to discover my middle swathed like a mummy in what seemed to be yards of gauze. Several hours later the orderly, who resembled Norm on the TV comedy, *Cheers,* transferred me to a gurney and wheeled me down the hall. He left me in a tiled room with a drain in the floor. I spent a half hour absolutely bored and wondering why I was there. Eventually the younger and more attractive of the two nurses attending me came in and disrobed me. This was embarrassing, but I seemed to be the only one having a problem with it. I pulled my gown across my lap as she had me sit up and began to unwrap the bandaging. When only a large gauze pad remained, she held it against my stomach while I lay down on my back. Then she carefully peeled off the pad.

Raising up onto my elbows, I was horrified to see three large open wounds left wide open without even an attempt at stitching. In the largest I could look right down into my vitals—a sight I'd never desired. My doctor came in and I asked why he hadn't sewn me up. "Why can I see my guts?" The surgeon explained he had to leave me open so he had access to the infected area for ongoing cleaning. I'd never heard of anything like this, but it didn't seem like the kind of thing I could effectively argue about in my condition. The nurse brought him a gallon jug of hydrogen peroxide. He had me lay back down and had the nurse hold my shoulders to the table. "This may hurt," he told me, and then he poured the cold liquid directly into my three wounds. He was right. It did hurt. The wounds erupted into foaming brown volcanoes. Even while trying not to scream, I still managed amazement at the foaming Vesuvius pouring out of me and down onto the floor. I was like the grossest science fair project ever.

We were to repeat this delightful activity every single day for the next two weeks. To keep things interesting, on a number of occasions he would reach inside me with forceps and pull out tissue killed by the infection. The pain in these sessions was off the charts. I would scream and only the fear of causing myself internal injury would keep me still as he probed and pulled. The nurse let me squeeze her hand through the worst of my agonies. This disgusted my doctor who scowled at her and sneered in English, "I will call you Nurse Pity." She cringed a bit but never failed to show compassion.

One day Norm the orderly took me to a new room. The older sterner nurse came in and wheeled over a large machine. On an adjustable arm this machine had a curved array of lights. She unwrapped my bandages and positioned the light over my gaping wounds. She indicated I needed to avert my eyes, turned on the machine bathing my stomach in a warm and intense light, and left the room. The sensation on my belly was not altogether unpleasant. It felt soothing and warm like the sun on your skin when you're at the beach. Of course I wasn't on sand, I was on a hard metal gurney, but in Outer Mongolia you take what you can get. Outside the window of my hospital room, snow covered the city and temperatures dropped into the teens, so I was inclined to try and enjoy the warmth. After a long time had passed, I began to grow concerned they'd forgotten me. The area receiving the light therapy was beginning to feel sunburnt. I decided someone needed a reminder. I began to call out, *Pozhaluista* (pa-ZHAL-sta— Russian for please) softly at first and then with increasing volume. This went on for five minutes or so, and then I began to practically scream it. The nurse finally returned and immediately shut off the machine. When she redressed my wounds and helped me back into my gown I noticed my skin hurt. My nurse called for Norm the orderly, and he redeposited me in my room. Within a couple of hours my skin had blistered and bubbled from mid-thigh to belly button. It was a deep angry pulsating red. The Russians had fried my body with ultraviolet light. (When did the War stop being Cold?)

My bed made sleep almost impossible. The hospital beds were about a foot too short for my 6' 4" frame. The nurses had extended mine with the addition of a short dresser and a pillow at the foot end to accommodate my freakish length. Now I had burns so painful I was only able to lie on my back. The merest brush against my skin made me gasp in pain and further complicated attempts at sleep. The next day, when Norm again attempted to steer me into that room, I protested vigorously. Using my arms to grab the door frame I shouted, "*Nyet! Nyet! Plocca macheen!*"

(Russian for "No! No! Bad machine!") over and over until the nurse came. I had almost no Russian vocabulary, but I understood she was trying to sweet talk me back under the light machine. I continued with my emphatic and simple refusal in Russian. She was offended I was defaming the device and told me repeatedly that it was a good machine. I kept showing her my burns and eventually she relented. Victorious, I felt like Caesar on his triumphal return from the Gallic wars as Norm wheeled me down the hall to my room.

With Louise back in the United States, frantic at the lack of news on my condition, I found myself lonely, bored, depressed, and struggling to keep from despair. The infection was making me very ill indeed. Though my doctors tried to hide the truth from me, I picked up on clues they were increasingly concerned about my condition. I began to feel I would not be leaving this hospital except in a box. I was thinking often of the hillside several miles eastward where my son Jedidiah's tiny grave lay under a blanket of snow. I increasingly felt a second Hogan grave would soon be joining his. I wrote out my Last Will and Testament and hid it in the drawer of my bedside table under my Bible.

I received a stream of visitors, almost all foreign missionaries, who tried to keep my spirits up. They actually formed a rotation to make sure I never went a morning or afternoon without company. The clinic had resumed their ban on Mongolian visitors, but my friends would come to my window to talk to and pray for me. Mats, a Swedish missionary and former teammate, brought his television and VCR to alleviate my boredom. He brought stacks of movies recorded from Swedish television. I remember a lengthy movie about an old man who lived by himself in a cabin in the woods. I watched the entire thing. Magda, a Dutch nurse working with street children, brought me the novel *Gai-Jin* by James Clavell. I really enjoyed the story of

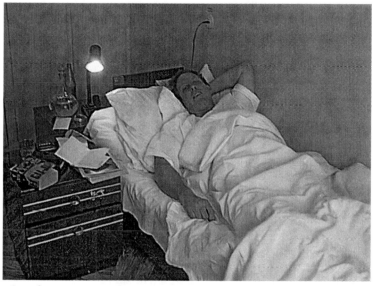

this foreigner in Japan until the disembowelment scene involving a sword. Finding this far too close for comfort, I wasn't able to resume reading for several days. A substitute diversion for long books was shouting out "Norm!" and waving just like the characters on *Cheers* whenever Russian Norm passed my door. He seemed puzzled by this, but evidentially enjoyed working the ward *where everybody knows your name.*

Even my surgeon tried to cheer me up. We had a tense interaction when he came to examine me and demanded I lay on my side to allow the wounds to drain. I angrily pointed out his hospital had burned me so badly I was unable to lie on my side. He replied, "Brian, you will lie on your side or you will become (pausing to struggle for words) a giant cave of pus." I immediately rolled painfully onto my side but angrily glared at him for his lack of compassion. To make amends, the next day he spent the entire afternoon with me. He brought a guitar and several videotapes. He treated me to renditions of songs by Dire Straits, his favorite rock band, and then we spent two hours watching home movies of his rafting trips on unexplored Siberian whitewater rapids. He had been the medical guy for several expeditions. His English commentary on what we were watching was both exciting and depressing. In too many of his stories, some of his companions never made it home, the river killing them by drowning or in some other manner. My missionary visitors informed me this same doctor had yelled at them on their way in to see me, "Your friend is very sad. This is not good. You must cheer him up!" We had a good laugh about this. So it was cheering.

The hospital food was uninspiring, to say the least. It reminded me of the English language sign in the Czech restaurant, "Our food will leave you nothing to hope for!" Mostly it was devoid of flavor and overcooked, but the worst thing for me was the over-prevalence of beets. I loathe beets! I mounted a campaign to ask for *blini* (crepes) whenever they scolded me to eat more. They refused and said that it was impossible in a hospital. I kept on being a dissident on the subject. I felt like a little *refusnik*. Our friend and partner Maria eventually managed to smuggle in Swedish pancakes for me during her morning visit. I relished every bite as I filled my shrunken stomach with those wonderful crepes. It felt wickedly wonderful to have received such contraband in my medical gulag. An hour later, my nurse wheeled the meal cart into my room and was beaming as she uncovered my lunch tray. *Blini!* I felt horrible. They had caved and filled my request, and I didn't have room to eat even one. I waited until she'd gone and then, for the first time since my second surgery, I stood up and walked. I slowly carried the much begged-for *blini* I couldn't bear to eat over to my toilet and flushed my shame away.

On my 15th day in intensive care, Magda had the morning visit shift. She told me she strongly suspected the antibiotics I was taking were ineffective. By this point we knew a strain of Staphylococcus that had been living inside of me for years was attacking my body. Louise and I had both picked it up while lifeguarding in Las Vegas during our first year of marriage. It caused a few painful pimples each year, usually on the inner thigh, but other than that had never bothered us much. The surgery had given the bacteria the opportunity it was waiting for, and it kicked into high gear. Now this tiny bug was threatening my life. Magda said Dr. Bob had left her some Ciprofloxacin, a potent, newer antibiotic, but she suspected the proud Russian doctors would refuse anything offered by a foreign nurse. She had been trying to figure out how to give it to them. I immediately thought of one of my YWAM coworkers working as a medical doctor in an

Ulaanbaatar hospital. Dr. Brad could easily call my surgeon as a colleague and offer him the Cipro. Magda agreed
and left immediately to put this subterfuge into motion.

Dr. Brad was more than game. He called my surgeon to
discuss his American patient. My doctor immediately told
him my infection was immune to medication and he felt
my survival was in jeopardy. Dr. Brad asked him if he
could send some Ciprofloxacin. My surgeon agreed and
urged Brad to do so without delay. Brad later told me the
relief was palpable across the phone lines. Dr. Brad immediately called Magda and she walked back to the clinic with
the Cipro. She said the doctor looked momentarily confused at the impossibly short time it had taken to reach
him, but decided not to think too deeply about it. My doctor put me immediately on this new antibiotic. Within
two days the infection was gone and I felt life returning.
On the morning of my seventeenth day in their care, the
medical staff announced they were releasing me. Too
much time had passed for my open wounds to accept su-
tures, so I would need to travel wrapped in bandages like
a partial mummy. My surgeon explained the wounds
would gradually heal from the inside outward, or from the
bottom up, in a process called *granualization.* Yuck! Yet,
the existence of this process further proved the human
body is a miracle.

My actual release went surprisingly quickly. Friends
arrived with a car to take me to the train station. Mats had
agreed to accompany me and carry my bags all the way to
the airplane. My surgeon came in with final instructions,
a jar containing my appendix, and a request I mail him

Mats took me to Ulaanbaatar on the train and got me onto the airplane.

Dire Straits sheet music. He requested that I present my appendix for examination by American doctors to vindicate his decisions in my case. When I thanked him this avowed atheist declared, "Your God saved you." The many visitors praying for me had not escaped his notice. The entire medical staff gathered in the wide hallway outside my room. Each gingerly took turns lightly hugging me goodbye. The Head Nurse gave a short speech in memorized English. "Thank you for coming, Brian. You are the princess of our hospital." It took superb self-control not to laugh. She then ceremoniously presented me with the hospital bill. Seventeen days in intensive care and two operations, not to mention expensive experimental machinery, cost me a whopping $320. I was able to pay off my bill in cash from my wallet. It was obvious my U.S. currency was a welcome sight.

The trip home was a bit of a blur. Both movement and sitting still brought their own aches and pains, and knowing gauze was the only thing between my guts and the floor added an exaggerated care to all my movements. When the flight attendant on my Seoul to San Francisco leg, asked me what was wrong, I lifted my shirt and told her I'd had abdominal surgery and the wounds were open. She immediately upgraded me to first class. When I mentioned the man behind me was my helper she upgraded him as well. I had met this guy, an executive with *Habitat for Humanity*, in the Korean airport. His kind offer to carry my bags had just paid an unexpected dividend. When I disembarked in San Francisco, I actually left the airport and took a cab to the commuter terminal. My father had flown his private plane up from Los Angeles in order to fly me home to Humboldt County. This tangible and uncommon expression of his concern and love touched me deeply.

Finally reunited with my relieved family and back in my own home, I was unable to immediately plunge back in to the work of running two ministry training schools. My condition forced me to take it easy and stay home. Since I was back on U.S. soil on November 7th, I insisted on going to the polls so I could vote for George W. Bush. (Hey, if it'd been Florida my vote would have made a huge difference!) I had dressings that needed changing and a lot of healing to do. One amazing provision I received was a male nurse for home healthcare on-demand. Bo Johnson was one of our students in the Frontier Mission Disciple-ship Training School. He was also a registered nurse and his school work duty changed to nursing me. Under his skillful and compassionate care, I made a quicker than ex-pected recovery. Within a month of my return I had only a few mementos of one of my closest brushes with death: a slimmer physique (having lost 30 pounds), three scars on the right side of my belly (one of them resembling a saber slash), and a wide deep brown swath of skin left behind when the burns healed. For an entire year this 18 inch wide stripe across my torso made me look as if I'd wrapped myself in the flag of a country whose national colors were pink and russet.

The staph infection had one last hurrah. Six weeks af-ter I returned home, with both training schools graduated and our kids out on Christmas break, our family had driven nine hours south to spend the holidays with my mom and stepfather in Atascadero, California. On New Year's Eve, just hours before the start of the new millen-nium (yes, I remember we celebrated a year earlier, but technically 1/1/2001 is the correct date), my largest wound site burst open. My skin had just barely completed healing and closing over it. Louise and Mom rushed me over to the Twin Cities Hospital Emergency Room where they cleaned me out and started me on powerful antibiot-ics. The miracle drug took a couple days to kick in, delay-ing our return home, but this time I was on the mend for good.

My late friend and mentor, Dr. Ralph D. Winter, founder of the U. S. Center for World Mission, became convinced near the end of his time on earth that microbes and viruses were agents and tools of the kingdom of darkness and combatting disease was part of our holy Kingdom calling and mission. At least twice these microscopic terrorists were the Enemy's suicide bombers—sent to blow me out of the battle permanently. Over lunch recently my friend, Dr. James Dunn, asked me which of all the accounts in this book were actually the most life threatening. After a couple minutes of me puzzling this out aloud, he rather authoritatively provided the answer: post-op staphylococcus infection in Mongolia, and malaria contracted up in Mozambique. Both microscopic, and both were only barely defeated by new breakthroughs in medical science and prayers that went up for me from all over the planet. I find myself forced to the conclusion that Ralph was right and this battle is an almost unrecognized front in the war we followers of Jesus have enlisted in. One day soon, Satan, Death and the Grave are diving into the Lake of Fire. I look forward to witnessing the tossing of the last of our still undefeated invisible and deadliest enemies into final annihilation alongside their Generals.

R

R is for Reckless

(Spring 1980)

There are certain queer times and occasions in this strange mixed
affair we call life when a man takes his whole universe for a vast
practical joke.

—Herman Melville

The last half of my senior year I felt I'd finally gotten things figured out, at least in regards to
school. I was doing well academically, and the
California Honor Society had just recognized it. I was enjoying traveling and singing in Crescenta Valley High
School's excellent choir. And for the past two years I'd
been part of a really wonderful crowd of friends. My private internal life was a hot mess, but that's a different
story—one for which only Jesus could write a happy ending.

If asked at 18 years of age what the most important thing in life was, I would've only had one answer: friends. My group of friends shared an interest in rock music, and in particular, a band called *Mary Poppinz. Mary Poppinz*  was a local glam rock band that had actually been getting gigs at clubs and parties. The year before they'd been a metal band called *Grim Reaper.* Three of my buddies, Matt, Mark, and Greg, were in the band. Greg and I had been inseparable friends since beginning high school. During our sophomore year we met freshmen Matt and Mark, and they adopted us into their crowd. The four of us formed the core of our group, but there were eight other kids who regularly hung with us, ranging in age from 15 to 20. What made this group really stand apart from the pack at CVHS was the fact none of us smoked or messed with drugs. Like Strider in *Lord of the Rings,* most of my friends looked foul and felt fair.

Mark was the lead guitarist and a potential teen idol with his long blonde hair and almost pretty looks. Resembling teen-idol Leif Garrett (who'd been my best friend in first grade in Burbank), Mark oozed cool. His divorced dad was my P. E. coach, and Mark and his siblings lived with their alcoholic mother. Mark had his issues, but he was always fun. He was a sneaky prankster who enjoyed stirring things up.

Matt and Mark

Matt was the band's bassist. At 16 he was already 6'4", and his slender towering frame ended in a mop of cascading red hair that spilled over his shoulders. He was by far the most intense about the music, taking weekly bass lessons at the local music shop. Matt's sole dream and goal was rock star status.

Greg, the drummer, was short, only 5'4", with long brown hair and a carefully crafted persona of cool. He pulled it off—I thought he was the coolest being on the planet. He and I had spent the previous summer at my aunt's house in Newport Beach bodysurfing the days away. Even during the school year, most weeks included at least one sleepover at his house or mine. He lived in a guesthouse behind the swimming pool in the backyard of his wealthy family's home, so we preferred his place to mine.

We all worked together, more or less, at three businesses across from each other on Foothill Boulevard, all owned by the Dundee family. Greg and I washed dishes at *Dundee's Scotch Mist* restaurant. Matt and Mark worked across the street at *Record World*, a music store owned by Mark Dundee, my boss's 16 year old. An older son owned *Sherlock's* discotheque adjoining *Record World*. All four of us minors worked illegally at *Sherlock's* as needed, mostly keeping its popular bar stocked.

Between hanging out at school, at work, and most of our free time, we were pretty much always together. We even spent a number of nights all sleeping over at Mark's house. His brother and sister would sometimes have sleepovers concurrent with ours, and Mark's mother would blearily wake hung-over to a house littered with sleeping teenage bodies. Other nights found us sleeping at Don's house. Don was a new member of the crowd whose almost spherical head had earned him the moniker, *Basketball Head*. Don worked at *Straw Hat Pizza*. Our entire crowd would show up late on Friday night and help him close up. Our help mainly consisted of running around and playing games and baking up a bunch of pizzas in guitar shapes. Then we'd stay up most the night eating pizza and watching movies at Don's house. Don's parents were early adopters of the videotape recorder, and their VCR was our crowd's favorite appliance. Don's mom, a Jesus follower, had the added attraction of being incredibly tolerant of Don's new friends.

By March of 1980, we were already a couple of months deep into a war of practical jokes. Mark, of course, had started the whole thing by inciting Matt to participate in pranking me. They had taken a goldfish from the science classroom and smashed it into my math textbook. By the time I discovered it, the squished mess had partially dried and managed to glue 15 or 20 pages together.

Before I had a chance to retaliate, several of the gang targeted Greg. They waited until Greg's family went to their Lake Arrowhead cabin for a weekend and then snuck into Greg's guesthouse where they wrapped every single object in newspaper like hundreds of presents. When Greg returned home he called me, and after having cleverly determined I was a fellow victim and not a culprit, he pitched his plan for revenge.

Friday night we all piled into Matt's car for a late-night trip to the city park at the bottom of Dunsmore Ave. We liked to play hide-and-go-seek at night amongst its trees and bushes. We'd usually end up by staging a Chinese Riot, a game that consisted of gathering at the edge of the park behind somebody's house on Forestglen Drive and all shouting in unison in simulated Chinese until someone yelled at us or we heard police sirens. Then we'd run away.

On this particular Friday night, Greg and I had something different planned. We slipped out of the park during the hiding phase and made our way to a nearby donut shop. It was open late, and we asked the guy for a bag and some napkins. He shrugged and handed them over. He just worked there, so this was no skin off his teeth. Greg and I went around the back and lifted the lid of the dumpster. I gave Greg a boost and he went dumpster diving. He found a number of stale doughnuts that still looked just fine in the filthy bottom of the garbage. As he handed them out to me, I carefully placed four doughnuts into the bag. Greg climbed out. We ran back to the park's parking lot and put the bag on the front seat of Matt's car. We quickly rejoined the game without anyone having missed us.

Finally, one of the park's neighbors threatened to call the cops, and we ran to pile into Matt's car. Mark and Don yelled "shotgun", and took the coveted front seat next to Matt while Greg and I groused about having to get in back. They discovered our bag of doughnuts right away. We protested they were ours and asked them to hand the bag back to us. They laughed and each grabbed a doughnut, saying something about "finders keepers". As they devoured *our* doughnuts, Greg and I bit our knuckles to keep from laughing and tipping them off. Mark glanced back at us and immediately realized something was up. He lowered his doughnut and glared at us, but said nothing. Mark's only consolation was watching Matt and Don continue getting pranked even worse than we'd pranked him. As they wiped the frosting and donut crumbs from their lips, Greg and I burst out in hysterical laughter and barely managed an explanation of the origin of those doughnuts. Suddenly, stolen doughnuts were not sweeter than the average variety.

The war was on!

The next offensive came against me. Mark hung four large and very dead trout on the coat hooks in my school locker. The idea was that I would be surprised to find them as I grabbed my books for weekend homework at the end of the school day. However, it was a three day holiday weekend. So, having no homework assignments, I headed straight home without a visit to my locker. On Tuesday, when school resumed, a hideous smell greeted me in the hallway a dozen yards before reaching my locker. The stench grew the closer I got, and my eyes almost watered as I dialed in my combination. The rotted fish had dripped fluids all over my notebooks and homemade paper bag covers of my textbooks. At least school property escaped with only surface staining. The putrid odor lessened over time, but only graduation finally delivered me from that aroma.

To pay them back, I sprayed an entire bottle of my mom's *White Shoulders* perfume (which I loathed and wanted out of our home) through the vents into Matt's locker and nervously waited for his response. He didn't say a word, but I knew something was coming. Meanwhile, silly and unmemorable pranks were flying fast and furious in every direction amongst our crew. Many involved ditching someone and leaving them to make their way home on their own. It got so you tried never to let anyone out of your sight.

One night we were again *helping* Don to close up *Straw Hat.* Everyone except Don was playing a game of chase all over the property. There was this new kid named Binky. Reflecting back, I'm sure that's not what his parents named him, but it's the only name for him I ever knew. Greg told me, "Binky's on the roof." There was a ladder set into the outside back wall of the restaurant. I quickly clambered up knowing Binky had no escape from the rooftop. Just as I reached the top of the ladder, two of my friends on the roof tipped a 30-gallon trash can filled with pizza sauce over my head. I clung to the ladder as chunky red sauce inundated me from above. I was completely drenched and looked like a victim from *Attack of the Killer Tomatoes.* Knowing what was to come, everyone had gathered well outside the splash zone in the parking lot below me. They were all laughing hysterically. Remembering Greg, my best friend, had urged me to go up the ladder, I figured he was a traitor and the practical joke was his doing. Leaping off the bottom of the ladder, I threw my arms around Greg. While bear-hugging him, I rubbed as much of the sauce as I could onto Greg. He screamed and cursed, but there was nothing he could do. Both of us were covered. Everyone laughed even harder. Afterward, I learned Mark had cooked up the entire scheme. Greg had only been his not-entirely-unwitting pawn.

Still, the experience drove a temporary wedge into my friendship with Greg. When the others suggested playing a joke on Greg at school the next day, I was in. While class was in session, we removed a coin operated feminine hygiene dispenser from the girls' restroom. I knew Greg's locker combination. It was a quick job to slide the machine into the narrow locker where it fit perfectly. We positioned books underneath the tall vending machine so it leaned forward against the locker door when we slammed the locker shut. When the bell rang we all made sure we were hanging out in the vicinity when Greg ran up to open his locker. It was even more impressive than we had imagined. Greg turned his head to talk with us as he

opened the locker. Unseen by Greg, the white metal machine tipped forward and fell to the floor. It landed with a
loud crash and flew open upon impact spewing unmen-
tionables across the hall. Everyone in the crowded hallway
was pointing and laughing, and Greg was humiliated and
livid. I should've known payback was coming.

The next day after school I went to the bike rack to unlock my Schwinn 10-speed for the ride home. My route
was a mile and a half, almost all of it down the steep hill of
La Crescenta Avenue. I threw my leg over the bike and
began to pedal down Prospect Avenue. When I reached
the corner, I turned downhill onto La Crescenta without
braking. Picking up speed, I enjoyed the breeze generated
as I sailed along. The stoplight on Montrose Avenue
turned green ahead of me. Though I didn't need to stop, I
applied the brakes to slow down through the intersection.
It was a hideous sensation to feel the handbrakes pull all
the way back with no tension at all. I was hurtling downhill on a busy street with no brakes whatsoever!

I looked down at my handlebars and could see someone
had disengaged both handbrakes by flipping out a little
metal doohickey. I could clearly see what I needed to do to
restore braking power, but I was completely unable to release my grip while traveling at such speed. Across the intersection I hurtled. I began to worry about the
approaching stoplight at Honolulu Avenue. If I didn't
catch the signal while it was green, it could be the end of
me. I could see the light ahead glowing red as the five short
blocks sped by. With just a half block until disaster, the

light changed to green, and the last car cleared the intersection moments before I shot through.

Without time to feel relieved, I realized I had just four long blocks to figure out how to stop before I reached the light at Shirlyjean Street where I lived. I certainly couldn't keep plummeting down the street all the way into downtown Glendale and hope to survive. I came to the conclusion I needed a controlled wreck. I began to scan for a yard I wouldn't mind crashing into along my side of the road. I needed a driveway I could use to clear the curb and an ivy or ice plant covered hill to break my fall. The fact that these were popular and trendy ground covers in Southern California during my childhood improved my chances greatly. Spotting a fast approaching yard that fit the bill, I put my escape plan into motion. I made a slight right turn into the graded driveway, and my bicycle became airborne as I hit the slope. I used my legs to kick the bike away from me so I wouldn't be landing on it. I came down hard on the ivy-covered slope. The thick tangled vegetation slowed me down as I tumbled wildly out of control.

Miraculously, as I got to my feet and took stock, beyond a few scrapes and contusions, both the bicycle and I had survived. As I walked my bike, its front wheel out of alignment, my anger grew with my growing suspicion Greg was behind this attempted assassination. I began to call my other friends as soon as I got home. Through the interrogation of shocked friends, I quickly established Greg had in fact disconnected my brakes, and when I described the disastrous results, everyone joined in on my anger toward him. Before long the group was considering ostracizing Greg.

Eventually, my best friend called me filled with worry and remorse. Greg explained he'd only intended to frighten me with his practical joke. He said, "I was sure you'd have to brake multiple times between the bike racks and the hill. I thought at worst you'd have to put down your feet to stop." Soon I'd forgiven my best friend, and I began phoning around to call the attack dogs off Greg. The scare rippling through our entire group of friends after my near-death careen down the hill on a brakeless bike forced an armistice to the practical joke war.

S

S is for Seawater

(1996)

*You hurled me into the depths, into the very heart of the seas, and
the currents swirled about me; all your waves and breakers swept
over me. . . . The engulfing waters threatened me, the deep
surrounded me; seaweed was wrapped around my head. . . . But you,
Lord my God, brought my life up from the pit.*

—Jonah 2:3, 5-6 (NIV)

After we handed over the church in Erdenet to our
Mongolian disciples, we moved into my mother's
home for four months to give Louise a chance to
give birth to our fifth child. Peter Magnus Hogan was
born on August 10, 1996, and six weeks later we moved to
our new posting on the Caribbean island of Barbados. The
entire family was excited about an opportunity to warm
up after 3 ½ years in the icebox of Asia.

So within the week of our arrival, we went off in search of the perfect beach. We followed directions given by one of our new Barbadian friends and parked alongside the coastal road on the east side of the island. A short walk through some trees brought us out onto an incredible strand of white sand fringed with palms. It really looked like something off a travel poster. Louise had Peter against her chest in his sling, I got our three girls situated on beach towels, and Molly and Melody began to play in the sand. Alice, our five-year-old, saw me headed for the warm Caribbean water and ran alongside me begging for a swim.

The two of us ran in holding hands, thoroughly enjoying this water that took no getting used to—so unlike our native Pacific waters. We quickly got into water beyond Alice's depth, so I lifted her onto my shoulders. I continued to walk out until I was in water up to my chest. As I walked, I stepped off into a low spot in the sand and lost my footing. I tried to get back to where I could stand up, but I was suddenly in over my head. I paddled with my head and shoulders above the water and Alice was fine, but I quickly became puzzled by my inability to find shallower water. As I paddled toward shore, I actually noticed the beach seemed to be slipping further and further away. We were in a riptide. I told Alice to hang on tight and I began to swim with everything I had. The best I could do was to stay in place. I've never been a particularly strong swimmer, and I began to tire rather quickly. As the water pulled us further away from shore, I waved frantically and got Louise's attention.

Louise ran down to the surf-line and quickly realized the trouble we were in. I saw her run back and leave Peter with Melody and strip off the sling and her shirt. By this point I was frightened and praying like crazy. As Louise began to run back towards the surf, a tall black Rasta-man with dreadlocks and a live monkey on his shoulder came up to her. I could see him talking to her and gesticulating, but couldn't hear a thing. I was getting so tired I couldn't keep paddling. I told Alice to hold her breath, and went down to the bottom and bounced back up. The bottom was only about two feet under my feet, but that was no help to us other than allowing a brief respite each time I bounced off it. Seeing how quickly the shore continued to rush away, I began to think this was the end for both of us. I called out to God again and again.

Suddenly I noticed Louise and the Rasta-man were both flailing their arms over their heads in a choreographed manner. At first I couldn't decide what they were trying to communicate, but I quickly realized they were telling me to swim to my right, rather than straight toward shore. With the last of my strength, I turned sideways and paddled several strokes toward the right. That was all it took!

We were out of the riptide and bobbing in water that wasn't trying to kill us. The problem was now my exhaustion. Completely spent by this point, I had to keep asking Alice to hold her breath as I bounced off the bottom to make any progress at all toward shore. My arms and legs might as well have been sandbags. Once it was clear to those onshore we were out of the riptide's grip, Louise swam out and took Alice from me. Unencumbered, I was able to make my own slow way to shore and collapse onto the sand.

By the time Louise reached the beach with Alice, the Rasta-man was gone. Melody said that he'd introduced them to his monkey and then walked off through the trees. Louise and I later speculated he may have been an angel sent to us in our dire need.

T

T is for Tunnel

(Summer 2009)

In his hand are the depths of the earth, and the mountain peaks belong to him

—David in Psalm 95:4 (NIV)

Twenty-five years of marriage is quite an accomplishment. Louise and I decided this milestone deserved significant commemoration. YWAM's main Norwegian base had invited us to teach church planting from June 15th through the 19th. The class was in Grimerud, close to Lillehammer, host of the 1994 Winter Olympic Games. Since I'd be teaching on June 16th, our wedding anniversary, I asked my lovely bride to accompany me to Norway. We booked our flights so we'd have an extra week after my teaching. Planning and anticipating together what we'd do with that week was almost as much fun as actually doing it.

Wanting to get as comprehensive a taste of Norway as possible within our time constraints, we booked something called *Norway in a Nutshell.* This was a loop tour by train, ferry, and bus. It would take us through deep and scenic fjords, dra-  matic mountain valleys, past spectacular waterfalls, and across the snowy roof of Norway. We'd be able to hop on and off the tour wherever we wanted to spend some extra time. We chose hotels located one stop beyond those recommended by the tour organizers, all of which were in crowded tourist towns. The train would empty out and we'd stay put. A few miles later we'd disembark alone to quiet and crowd-free accommodations and environs to

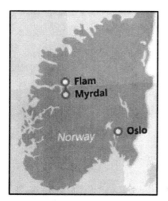

Flåm Railway route

explore on foot. One piece of the nutshell we especially looked forward to was the Flåm Railway. Starting from the mountain station at Myrdal, this scenic train snakes down to Flåm via the longest and deepest fjord in Europe, the Sognefjorden. The journey goes through the steep and narrow Flåm Valley with vistas of towering waterfalls and lofty snow-capped peaks and takes only 40 minutes if you do not stop along the way.

Both Louise and I derived immense enjoyment from the week of teaching and interaction with the eager students and gracious YWAM staff. In the evenings we conversed, coached, and played games with our new friends. During a game night with some of the staff, we discovered our favorite board game: *Ticket to Ride*. It was ironic spending an evening building imaginary train routes across the United States just before embarking on a Norwegian train journey.

On Saturday June 20th, our hosts dropped us off at the train station in Hamer to begin our anniversary journey. The first leg of the trip took us to Myrdal, the beginning and end station of the famous Flåm Railway. Everyone else had booked hotels in Myrdal, but Louise and I began our trip on the scenic railway and disembarked at the next stop. Vatnahalsen Station was a tiny affair compared to Myrdal, less than a mile behind, but it had the advantage of seclusion, no traffic (as access was solely by rail) and only a single structure beside the train station: the *Vatnahalsen Hotell.*

It was summer in Scandinavia, land of the midnight
sun. So, after arrival, check in, and a late dinner, we decided to take advantage of the bright 9 P.M. daylight and
go for a long walk. We headed further up the valley from
the hotel on a trail roughly paralleling, but out of sight of,
the train tracks we'd be taking onward the next day. After
about 2000 feet, our trail looped downward and intersected the tracks. Louise felt it was high time to head back
to our inviting hotel room, so I suggested we follow the
tracks back, since we knew that they'd take us directly to
the station in front of the hotel. Walking between the rails
for about a quarter-mile, we came to a tiny station building on the right called Reinunga, not much more than a
trackside shelter from the elements. Just ahead loomed the

Vatnahalsen Tunnel. Note warning sign in blow-up view (bottom right)

opening of a tunnel. This was puzzling. We hadn't encountered a tunnel on our outward walk. We must have
missed it while on the trail while the train tracks were just

out of sight. Given how close we must be to the hotel, and seeing the tunnel was pointed in the right general direction, I suggested we take the shortcut through what must be a very short train tunnel.

We hadn't gone very far before the light began to fail. Quite soon we were walking hand-in-hand in pitch blackness. We continued on doggedly forward longer than we felt we should have had to. Just as Louise began to suggest we retrace our steps, we saw a glimmer of *the light at the end of the tunnel.* Much relieved, we picked up the pace only to discover the light was streaming in from a large floor-to-ceiling gap cut into the side of the tunnel and overlooking the gorgeous Flåm Gorge. Disappointed, but feeling the real end of the tunnel must be that much nearer, we continued on into the darkness. As we progressed, simply walking along the tracks became slow and difficult. Every few steps we'd stumble over the rails even though we were endeavoring to walk in as straight a line as possible. This went on for what became an absurdly long time. After about 30 minutes, we were both becoming frightened. Louise was fighting tears, and I was praying silently and singing praise songs to lighten the mood. We walked on and on, stumbling over and over, in darkness so absolute we seemed to be blind. It was almost beyond intolerable when a thrill of joy shot through me at the glimpse of light far ahead. Both sets of starved eyes took it in at once. Encouraged, we pressed forward toward the glow.

Upon reaching the exit, what we saw quickly dashed our overjoyed relief. We were stunned to find ourselves on a 15 yard ledge of a cliff between two tunnels. Louise finally quit holding back tears. I tried to console her, but I was feeling much the same way. Trapped, neither of us could bear the thought of returning the way we had come. Looking out from our ledge we had a view of a deep mountain valley with a huge waterfall and a river running along the bottom. This was a vista people would pay money to gaze upon and yet, the site was almost repulsive

to us—as trapped on our cliff as Rapunzel in her tower. I scanned the mountain rising above the tunnel mouth we'd just exited. I told Louise somehow the tunnel must have curved away from our hotel which must be just over the mountain. I considered whether we could scale the peak like the Von Trapp family, but the sheer sides and lack of a trail dissuaded me. We would not *Climb Every Mountain* this day. We were stuck.

I wanted to restore Louise's spirits, but couldn't think of anything cheerful. I told her even though the thought was horrible, we had to retrace our steps. This produced fresh tears. I prayed, "God please rescue us. Show me a way out of here." I opened my eyes and saw a chainsaw lying between the track and the cliff face. Shocked at seeing an expensive piece of equipment abandoned in the middle of nowhere, I looked around more carefully. Just beyond the chainsaw was a leather tool belt and, wonder of wonders, a hardhat with a light on the front! I breathed thanks to our Father for such an instant answer to my plea for help. I picked up the helmet and switched on the light. It worked! "Louise! Look what I found!" My wife looked up, taking in the sight of me with a lighted hardhat sitting on my head. Excited, I gushed, "There's a tool belt and chainsaw too. Someone just left them here. This light will make getting back through the tunnel a walk in the park."

"Brian, you can't take that hat. It belongs to the train man. What will he do if it's missing?"

"He'll have a train! He can easily go and get another hat. God gave this one to me. I asked Him for help and there it was. There's no way I'm leaving it here."

Louise looked a little worried, but the relief of having a way out of our situation overrode any moral qualms. We rejoined hands and headed back into the terrible tunnel. The light, though quite small, illumined really well, and we were able to walk at full speed without any tripping or hesitation. Our spirits lifted immeasurably. We were going to survive this.

At what must've been halfway through the tunnel, we began to hear, softly at first, a growing noise that sounded like an underground waterfall. Louise mentioned it and said, "It's funny that it wasn't running when we came through here before." We paused to listen more closely to this odd intermittent cataract and both had the same terrible thought dawn at the same moment. This was no waterfall—it was an oncoming train!

I pulled Louise to the side and shouted, "Flatten yourself against the wall!" We both pressed our bodies and our faces as flat as we could against the rough rock wall of the tunnel. Somehow I had the presence of mind to reach up and flick off the light on my hardhat. Moments later, the tunnel filled with light and noise. A motored maintenance car with two workmen inside roared past us, two feet from our backs. It only took a few seconds and we were back in darkness as they rumbled around the bend. The car's passage made one startling thing very clear. This train tunnel curved around beneath the earth. Weird. I'd never considered the possibility of a twisting train tunnel.

Shaken, Louise and I collected ourselves and stepped back onto the tracks. I relighted the helmet and we continued on our way. What had taken almost forty minutes on our initial trip, we now covered in about ten. It was amazing how light sped things up. We reached the entrance to the tunnel and saw Reinunga Station ahead. What a welcome sight that humble little building was. I cannot think of a time in my life when I was more relieved. Opening the door to the station, I removed my miracle hardhat, turned off its lifesaving light, and laid it reverently on the bench for the train man to retrieve.

Louise and I talked about what to do. Facing out on the porch of the station, we could see our hotel's roof above the trees about ¼ mile away, but a marshy area separated us from it. I was for finding a shortcut across the marsh and heading straight to the hotel. Louise absolutely refused to consider another shortcut and insisted we follow the tracks all the way back to the hotel. Feeling a bit overdrawn in the relational bank, I decided not to argue.

By following the tracks we discovered they made a hairpin curve at valley's end, and this created almost parallel sets of tracks on opposite sides of the narrow valley. This odd and unforeseen roadway had confused me into thinking the tracks we'd hit led back to the hotel when they actually were heading away from it but in the same general direction. Even though our return walk was longer than it had to be, it wasn't long until we arrived safely back at Vatnahalsen Hotell. We went right to bed, more exhausted by the tunnel terror we'd endured than by our exertions.

The next morning after a wonderful breakfast, we boarded the train to continue our journey. Because the Flåm Railway is a special tourist route, the trip came with commentary in English. It wasn't long before we'd learned something about Vatnahalsen Tunnel which we'd explored the night before. At 2,890 feet in length, the tunnel spirals inside the mountain to cope with the 2,838 foot change in elevation along a mere dozen miles of track—Europe's sharpest subterranean twist. The track exits the tunnel onto an artificial shelf on a cliff which falls several hundred yards down, then continues on into another tunnel.

We were still traveling through the Vatnahalsen Tunnel in our unlit salon car when the recorded commentary ended and silence fell. Sitting next to Louise at our table in the darkness, I exclaimed, "Can you believe we walked all the way through this last night?" Just then we pulled out of the tunnel and into the light of the ledge where God had provided our *Helmet of Salvation.* An elderly couple seated across from us were staring with widened eyes and aghast looks at these obviously deranged and unhinged Americans. Almost immediately our car went dark again as it entered the next tunnel. Louise and I tried valiantly and unsuccessfully to stifle our giggles at their reaction.

U

U is for Underground
(1976)

If the Lord had not been on our side . . . the flood would have
engulfed us, the torrent would have swept over us, the raging waters
would have swept us away.

—David in *Psalm* 124:1, 4-5 (NIV)

Throughout the 1970s, my family lived in Oakmont Woods—an isolated and sleepy little neighborhood tucked up into the Verdugo foothills of
Glendale, California. The isolation was due to the only access—a single bridge that crossed a concrete jacketed river,
or what passes for a river in the Los Angeles area. Most of
the year, *The Wash,* as we called it, was a barely flowing
algae stain down the middle of the concrete riverbed. It
ran into a lake and sandy wetland that caught the runoff
before it hit the posh Oakmont Country Club. During our

infrequent rainstorms, it became a raging torrent. Although it was illegal to trespass in the wash, it was our playground. We slid down the slime on boogie boards, explored the subterranean storm channels that snaked beneath the streets of Glendale, heaved bowling balls and pumpkins off the bridge, hunted toads and snakes, harvested the volunteer pumpkins and squash from the swamp, built forts in the stunted trees and brambles, and waged rock throwing wars with other gangs of kids for possession of this wonderland.

Looking up The Wash from the bridge into Oakmont Woods.
The Baby Wash can be seen entering on the left.

The neighborhood of Oakmont Woods spread uphill like skirts over the mountain's legs. Our house was at the bottom—number 1052 on ShirleyJean Street. Pretty much the whole neighborhood drained downward across

ShirleyJean and into the cul-de-sac that formed the down-hill end of Dolorita Street. Whenever it rained, large quantities of water ended up rushing into this cul-de-sac equipped with a giant drain to channel the floodwaters into a small tributary of The Wash.

All the neighborhood kids called this the *Baby Wash.* Entry into the drain from the cul-de-sac was, for safety reasons, very wisely restricted by a barrier of welded rebar. How-ever, entry into the drain from its Baby Wash outlet posed no problem whatsoever. The outlet was a four feet diam-eter concrete tube that formed a perfect tunnel right up to the drain on the cul-de-sac. This culvert sloped upward from the wash toward the street for about two-thirds of its length. However, the final 10 feet was very nearly level. This change in angle formed a kind of lip in the conduit right where it began to run downhill. It was here—under-ground—the Oakmont Woods Junior Corps of Engineers tested their boyish mettle against the forces of Nature.

A group of us used to go around the neighborhood door-to-door collecting items for recycling. You could get a little cash if you collected enough aluminum cans and newspapers. Of course, then you had to talk your parents into taking you to the recycling center with all your accu-mulated treasure. So these items tended to build up in our garages. When rain had the audacity to try and spoil our free time, we would pile newspaper into our wagons and drag them down into the Baby Wash. The operation we were planning required a minimum of four guys, but that was never a problem.

By some bizarre chance, in our tween age group, Oakmont Woods had only boys—about 15 of them. My own family alone had added four boys, so we hadn't helped the statistics by moving in. Okay . . . there was one girl, Janice Weber. But Janice hardly counted as she loathed all of us with a pure and perfect hatred. She and her brother Marvin lived in the house at the base of the very cul-de-sac we planned to convert into Lake Oakmont. Marvin Weber, on the other hand, was a stalwart member of our gang. Besides Marvin and me, two of my favorite partners-in-crime were the Anglo-Americans Robert and Tim Chapman. Born in England, Robert was my best friend and worst influence. In 1972, when we moved into the neighborhood, the *Welcome Wagon* lady (wearing a pirate patch over one eye—I am not making this stuff up) had warned my mother to keep me away from Robert Chapman who was "bad news". I overheard this and ran over to introduce myself to this fascinating character before the nosy neighbor had even left our home. I'd just reread *Tom Sawyer*; so imagine my unbridled joy in discovering we moved in just two doors up from Huckleberry Finn! Robert turned out to be all that had been advertised—a source of scathingly brilliant ideas and constant trouble. The four of us made up the core of the gang, though other boys often joined us.

On dam building days, we'd form an assembly line from the mouth of the tunnel up to the lip where it leveled off. With a nice stream of water already running along the bottom of the tunnel, the boy at the top would begin laying newspapers into the flow of the water. As they became waterlogged and heavy, we added more layers as gradually a wet newspaper dam developed. In this manner, we would attempt to completely clog the tunnel as water built up above the drain, flooding the cul-de-sac and, with luck, Mr. Weber's lawn. (This very lawn was the agreed upon site for any neighborhood fistfights that were necessary. These were always a big draw, including an epic one between Robert and me soon after we met. But that's another story.)

It was great fun no matter what job you had; jobs varied between running back and forth through the tunnel, hunched over, carrying newspapers to the dam, or building the dam itself, trying to keep every bit of water from making its way down the tunnel. Of course, after an hour or two, the pressure of the water became enough to actually move the dam. When we felt this begin, we would scurry down the tube and get out of the way. What happened next made it all worthwhile. The remains of our dam would shoot out of the tunnel like a cannonball in a rush of filthy, frothy water. The hydraulic display would continue for five minutes or more as the cul-de-sac drained. It was magnificent. After the show, happy and exhausted and soaked to the skin, we'd drag our empty wagons home and head for hot showers, hot soup and television. Heaven!

It never occurred to any of us this was dangerous. During our final hydrology project, I was at the top with Robert constructing the dam. This one was turning out to be one of our best yet. The rainfall was heavy and we had managed to bring enough newspaper to completely fill the tunnel to the very top. The dam was so effective that literally nothing was leaking past in the channel between our soaked tennis shoes. Robert scurried down the tunnel to tell Marvin and Tim not to bring up any more newspaper. I stood just behind the dam proudly surveying our handiwork. I could hear the other three coming back up the tunnel to view our engineering masterpiece. It was at this precise moment I felt the dam begin to shift. I desperately pushed back against the wall of newspaper, but it was immediately obvious there was no holding this juggernaut back. I yelled to the others, "Get out! It's going to blow!" I immediately spun around and began to run down the tunnel as quickly as my bent-over stance would allow. My friends were slower to respond. I ran into Robert and started pushing him down the tunnel. My friends got the message and they began to move, but the dam was following me. When I later saw Indiana Jones chased by the giant ball, I knew what Indy was feeling.

As each of my friends cleared the end of the tunnel, they dove to the left—upstream in the small wash. From experience and observation we all knew you did not want to be in the path of what shot out of the tunnel. As I followed just behind Robert, leaping out of the culvert's mouth, the dam caught up with me. This incredible mass of soggy newspaper and water under pressure caught my right arm as I leapt to the left. The force carried me completely across the concrete wash and slammed me into the opposite wall. I fell to the ground right next to where the gusher was pounding into the wall. I crawled away as quickly as I could, toward my friends who were yelling and jumping around like lunatics. Noting I had somehow survived, they were able to fully embrace the glorious wonder of our creation. I was a bit too distracted by pain and shock at how close I'd come to destruction. As I took stock of my condition, I realized I was going to be very sore and bruised, especially on my right side. The wristwatch my grandfather had given me had been shattered against the concrete by the force of the burst dam. I felt grateful it wasn't my head. That last dam we ever constructed became a neighborhood legend. I'd often hear kids who hadn't been there telling the tale as if they had been. It was tangible glory I could wrap myself up in— like the blanket I snuggled in while Robert and I watched "Monty Python's Flying Circus" after our adventure.

V

V is for Vehicular

(1980)

"It's a dangerous business, Frodo, going out your door. You step onto the road, and if you don't keep your feet, there's no knowing where you might be swept off to."

—J.R.R. Tolkien, *The Lord of the Rings*

Since this story took place almost immediately following God's dramatic rescue of me from the misguided and disastrous rule of Brian Hogan into the paradise of His Rule and Kingdom, I need to start six days before the crash and tell you about the greatest evening of my life.

In early June 1980, I was about to graduate from Crescenta Valley High School, and I was living a triple life. I was one person with my mom at home, at least putting on a fraying facade of a good Methodist boy. At school I was

Author's Senior Picture

an honor student, editor of *The Ark*—Crescenta Valley High's poetry publication, touring with the choir, and I was accepted to Cal Poly San Luis Obispo, a deeply impacted university. My group of friends at school, in the words of Frodo Baggins, "looked foul and felt fair". They were in a glam rock band called *Mary Poppinz* and rarely drank and were drug-free, though most of our peers assumed otherwise. My neighborhood friends were a completely different story. We lived to get drunk and were miserable when our plans to buy or swipe alcohol fell through. Looking back, part of the need for inebriation was to dull the guilt from the compulsive "sins of the flesh" our booze-soaked, lowered inhibitions led us into. We seemed to swing wildly between poles of teen lust and extreme guilt, me most of all since my Sunday School encoding was still in place. Knowing my other worlds could never accept the truth I hid, I crawled out the bedroom window to feed my monster of iniquity several nights a week.

The strain of living with a constant cycle of violating my own principles, asking God to forgive me, and bargaining with promises to behave, breaking those promises—sometimes within hours—caused me to come to a place of almost complete breakdown. I had been fighting off increasingly powerful thoughts of ending my own life. I had just attended the funeral of a teen coworker and friend who'd hung himself in his closet, and I knew of a couple of suicides from school. So, these peer examples played into my thinking. My road seemed to be taking me further from any hope of heaven than even suicide would accomplish.

Don Trousdale

At about my lowest point, I went to find my friend from school, Don Trousdale. We all called him "Basketball Head" because his head was rounder than any in our gang. I really liked Don because he was simply kind and didn't play tricks and practical jokes like the rest of us. It didn't hurt he had the coolest job in the group as well. He worked at Straw Hat Pizza, and we used to all go to hang out while he closed up. We'd make funny pizzas in the shape of guitars we admired and other shapes I don't care to put into print. Then five or six of us would all go to Don's house and eat our pizza in front of movies (they had an early VCR), and fall asleep sprawled all over his family's living room floor and furniture. The thing that always amazed me was that his folks were cool with this.

So on this fateful day, I arrived at Don's house to find no one at home except his mom, Harriett, and she was in tears. I really liked her, so I pressed to find out what was wrong. She told me God had moved them to invest a lot of their money into renting the Glendale Civic Auditorium and bringing in the famous hippie evangelist, Lonnie Frisbee, who'd launched the Jesus People and Calvary Chapel Movements a decade earlier.[4] Harriet told me the first meeting the previous week had been almost empty, and she was feeling they had misheard God and made a huge mistake. Wanting to make Harriett feel better, I impetuously volunteered all of my friends to attend that evening. I told her Don was driving and she needed to tell him to pick us up when he returned. I set out immediately

---

[4] Just a few months before, on Mother's Day, 1980, John Wimber asked Lonnie Frisbee to come speak at his church in Yorba Linda. It literally changed history. Lonnie launched the Vineyard Movement, and through that, ended up again deeply impacting my life.)

on my Honda Express moped to gather Matt, Mark, Greg, Cori, and anyone else from our group I could find.

None of them wanted to go until I guilted them into it by reminding them how much we owed Mrs. Trousdale. We managed to show up in time to go into the auditorium as a group of six. Only Greg and I had any church background and none had any real relationship with God. Attendance had picked up and there were probably 150 people there. A Christian bluegrass band, Crystal River, opened with the first real worship experience of my life. Something happened to me as I sang. Looking back, I must have finally begun surrendering to the grace of God. I began to feel real hope for the first time in months. Then Lonnie got up and preached. I can't remember anything from the message except the excitement it produced in me. I knew I wanted in. After he finished, he called any who wanted to live this life to come forward and confirm it by taking communion. I had done this many times growing up in the Methodist Church, but this was different. This was a commitment. I went forward glowing with anticipation. All of my friends except Greg, my best friend, kept their seats. I got in line. Looking to the front of the queue, I watched Lonnie wordlessly give each person a wafer. Another guy was distributing little juice cups. When I reached the front Lonnie stared intently into my eyes and did something he hadn't done with anyone else. He reached up his hand holding my wafer and laid it on my head. He simply said, "I'm praying for your need." I felt like lightning struck my head. A surge went down and throughout my body. I was barely able to keep standing. I staggered away feeling sure everything had just changed and that God had somehow entered me. When I got back to my seat, a guy came running down from the back of the auditorium and grabbed me. This stranger blurted, "I just watched the Holy Spirit enter you like a lightning bolt!" My response was to hug him and say, "You saw it and I felt it. It must have happened!"

Over 3 decades later I got around to reading Lonnie Frisbee's autobiography, *Not by Might, Nor by Power*, and came across a similar experience. Lonnie's mother had crept into the back of a large meeting he was doing:

> " . . . she got an electrifying power that dropped down through the top of her head like white heat. It went through her whole body and lifted her out of her chair, and—that power brought her forward.
> She said, 'I don't remember even one foot touching the ground.'
> My mother received Jesus that night . . . ."

Over the course of the following six days, I led all of my friends into God's family, and we started a simple house church, which we called *Bible Study*. Our plan was to return for all the remaining Lonnie Frisbee meetings as well. The day before the meeting, I was riding my moped down a rather steep hill in La Crescenta, our foothill suburb of Glendale, California, and tried to brake for a red light on a section of road inexplicably covered with scattered gravel. My moped went into a careening upright slide that took me into the right curb and launched me through the air. My body's graceful flight toward a vacant lot stopped abruptly when I hit a rough creosote-soaked telephone pole. As I slithered to the ground I felt terrible pain in my left foot as well as impact trauma and scrapes all over the front of my body and hands. A guy who saw the crash from across the road came running across and asked if I was alright. I was trying to stand up and told him I thought I had a broken foot. He pulled my moped out of the road and said he was running to call an ambulance. I shouted, "No, we can't afford that. My mom is a nurse. Call her," and I gave him the number.

My mom was on the scene and helping me into the car within 15 minutes. My foot had already begun swelling. I had weeping sores in many places, and my hands were abraded and painful. But when she made the turn toward the Verdugo Hills Hospital Emergency Room, I told her to head home. An argument ensued because she had already determined I had a broken foot. The only way I was able to get her to delay taking me to the ER was to promise I would go the next night if nothing happened at the Lonnie Frisbee meeting. She didn't believe God healed anymore outside of medical intervention, but her suddenly transformed son was so convinced that she weighed the options and figured a day's wait would do no lasting harm.

I spent the next 26 hours laying on a couch with ice packs and aspirin as my foot swelled to melon size. Matt arrived by 6:00 to pick me up for the Lonnie Frisbee meeting. My friends had to support me as I painfully hopped down to his car, and again as I hopped to the auditorium and down to our seats. The packed hall was more full than the week before. The meeting followed the same pattern as previously. Worship that took me into the throne room of the Father, a message by Lonnie I loved but can't remember now, and communion in a line at the front which I had to hop down to on one foot. When I reached the front of the line and faced Lonnie he repeated exactly his action and words of the week before. "I'm praying for your need." Immediately I felt a current in my left foot. The pain, which had been throbbing from all the hopping, stopped at once. Without a word, I turned and walked normally back to my seat. My friend Mark had been in front of me at the communion line and asked, "Why does he only talk to you?" I turned to him in amazement and said, "I have no idea but my foot was just healed!" Mark then stomped on my foot to prove it wasn't. (See what I mean about Don being the nice one?) It didn't hurt at all. In fact, as I took inventory, my left foot felt better than any other part of me—with the exception of my heart and newborn spirit.

Soak me in your laundry and I'll come out clean, scrub me and I'll have a snow-white life. Tune me in to foot-tapping songs, set these once-broken bones to dancing.
—Psalms 51:7-8 (MSG)

W

W is for Whirlpool
(Summer 1968)

Inigo Montoya: *Fezzik, are there rocks ahead?*

Fezzik: *If there are, we all be dead.*

—The Princess Bride

The Summer of Love. There must've been something in the air. Everyone in California seemed to be grooving on something that summer. I was six and a half years old and grooving on camping.

The older generation just didn't get us. My grandparents, for example, were still jittery two days after I'd gotten this camping trip going with some far out adventuring (see *L is for Lost*). My mom was trying to be cool, but she *was* over thirty, and her oversight was bumming me out. Still, I managed to have a blast fishing, taking guided walks with rangers, playing with other children, sitting by campfires in the evenings, and enjoying my favorite activity: swimming.

When I burst out of the tent with my swimsuit on it was pretty clear what I was going to do next. My Nana Hogan insisted on accompanying me down to the swimming hole. I couldn't see why. I'd learned to swim in the Memorial Park pool in Blue Island, Illinois earlier that summer. My maternal grandparents had decided swimming lessons were a priority for this kid who couldn't stay away from water.

There was a stream flowing through our campground in the San Bernardino National Forest near Idyllwild. At the point where the watercourse intersected the paved access road into the camping area, a culvert beneath the roadway allowed the water to flow. The park service had constructed this culvert so that a pond formed on the upstream side of the road creating a wonderful swimming hole. Throughout the hot days, kids camping nearby filled this pool. I got to know a number of these swimmers through playing around the campground and making

Fishing at Idyllwild

frequent trips to the swimming hole. So I plunged in upon arrival, not even taking time to get used to the chilly stream water. Almost immediately, I was included in an ongoing splash fight. My grandmother took a seat on the edge of the road next to several other parent lifeguards.

After 15 to 20 minutes of strenuous watersport, I discovered a burning desire to have my Nana watch me while I stood on my hands underwater. I paddled over toward her roadside perch. An older boy stopped me and pointed to a spot next to the road where the water periodically swirled in a circle. He told me, "Stay away from that place. It's a whirlpool, and it will suck you down." I studied the surface of the water where he'd pointed. Most of the time it looked just like the rest of the swimming hole, sloshing with waves from all the splashing swimmers. Every once in a while, when that region experienced a moment or two of calm, the surface would begin to spin. This never seemed to develop into anything very impressive before wave action again disrupted it. I'd heard of whirlpools before, but they were huge and sucked ships down. This one seemed to be less interesting than what I created at home by unplugging our kitchen sink. During the time it took to swim over and get my grandmother's attention, the big kid's warning completely slipped my mind.

"Look, Nana. Watch me stand on my hands," I shouted as I scanned the water nearby for a kid-free spot where no one would knock me over.

I found an open spot just to my left and close by Nana's roadside perch. Just as I was going under to set up my handstand, I heard someone yell, "Stay away from there!" Almost immediately, the mouth of the culvert sucked me

in. With lightning speed belying her age and tiny physique, my grandmother grabbed my wrist with an iron
grip. The pull of the water rushing under the road was so
strong it almost pulled Nana in after me. I was completely
submerged, and her forearm was underwater. As she
clung to me, she screamed for help. By this point my body
was inside the corrugated metal culvert. My entire world
collapsed to the sound of water rushing by me and the
feeling of sharp pain in my arm where it pressed against
the culvert's edge. I felt another strong hand close around
my arm below my Nana's grip. A dad on the bridge had
come to my rescue. As he pulled with all his strength he
drew me from the maw of the deadly whirlpool. I don't
know how long it actually took, but it seemed like forever
to me. I swallowed a lot of water and was half-drowned
when they managed to pull me up onto the hot asphalt. I
didn't require mouth-to-mouth resuscitation, but I remember coughing up water for what seemed like forever.
My forearm was bleeding from the cut caused by the edge
of the culvert. A woman brought bandages and antibiotic
ointment to dress my wound. The blood didn't freak me
out. I bled a lot in childhood. I did not suffer from hemo-
philia, just recklessness and clumsiness. My grandmother
was wailing and crying, and the other adults clustering
around were so concerned for her they carried me to a
nearby picnic table and compelled her to sit down on the
bench and breathe deeply.

I have only three other strong memories of this event.
A nice man ran to his camper and brought me back a glass
of cold orange juice. This was a wonderful tonic after all

that turbid water. It functioned as a sort of miracle cure in terms of restoring my sense of well-being and zest for life. Another thing I remember is, upon recovery, I insisted on seeing where the culvert dumped out on the other side of the road. There was a kind of waterfall that ended with a smash on rocks six or seven feet below. I remember thinking how much that plunge would have hurt. The only other thing I remember is that the older boy who'd warned me of the impending danger came over and told me, "I told you so," in front of all those people. What a square!

The fateful camping trip ended on this note. Traumatized, my poor Nana and Papa insisted that we pack up and return to Burbank immediately. This time my mom didn't even try to argue. None of them had the heart to see what I'd get up to next in the wild.

My paternal grandparents never took another camping  trip. From this point on, they took me to resorts and fancy hotels but avoided Mother Nature. I continued to fish with my grandfather but only day trips to Ventura Pier and Castaic Lake Dam. Swimming was limited to the pool at their mobile home park. For the great outdoors, I'd have to rely on Mom and her parents, Nana Alice and Papa Jim.

X is for Xenophobia
(Fall 2007)

Anyone who describes Islam as a religion as intolerant encourages violence.

—Tasnim Aslam, Pakistan's Foreign Ministry spokesman

(The Pope's remarks) *"threaten world peace"* (and) *"pour oil on the fire and ignite the wrath of the whole Islamic world."*

—Mohammed Mahdi Akef, Egypt's Muslim Brotherhood

E gypt's searing sun seemed to sap the energy from my body as I entered the station at the southern terminus of Cairo's Metro. I'd already had a long morning training church planters deep within a secret compound in this Cairo suburb. Passionate about what I teach, I normally find the time I spend with trainees energizing. This week though, the climate and the tension generated by the populace's crankiness, due to Ramadan fasting and the covert nature of our training, was leaving me drained and listless. Yet I forced myself to leave the compound after lunch and get in some sightseeing. It would be criminal to waste a day in fascinating Egypt.

The Women's Car

The Metro station in Helwan was the end of the line. The train sat almost empty and I carefully chose a carriage permitting male commuters. On an earlier trip to Egypt I boarded one of the two carriages reserved for women and endured an excruciatingly embarrassing journey once I realized my mistake. Like running into a women's restroom without knowing it—it's something you only do once. As I boarded the train for this day out, I'm ashamed to admit I was overjoyed to see I would have the car to myself. I was not in the mood for smelly crowds or interaction with locals. I know missionaries are supposed to thrive on this stuff. Usually I seek out and enjoy cross-cultural interactions. This afternoon I was relishing the thought of a quiet and restful

journey to downtown Cairo's Sadat Station seventeen stops ahead. My destination was the famous Tahrir Square and the nearby Egyptian Antiquities Museum. Perhaps by arrival I'd be refreshed enough to tackle the museum's acres of mummies, canopic jars and sarcophagi.

After about 10 minutes, the train started up and began rumbling northward. I gazed languidly out the window as urban and desert scenery flashed by. The second stop,

Helwan University, was a crushing disappointment. Departing students packed the platform. As soon as the automatic doors opened, a flood began and continued until every available inch

Another day on the Cairo Metro. My friend's face obscured for reasons of security.

was filled with jostling pressing human flesh. My bench seat, thoughtfully designed to hold two rear ends, suddenly bore the weight of five as two students crushed in on either side of me and invited friends to sit on their laps. I actually felt ill-bred and impolite as I ignored those standing inches from my face pointedly eyeing my lap. My paradise had turned to purgatory.

Thinking things cannot possibly get worse is among the stupider thoughts one can entertain. Something almost always proves that premise to be erroneous. I had no sooner finished framing this thought in my mind when one of the lap sitters beside me asked, "Are you an American?"

Argh! I hate this question—especially in the Middle East. One never knows where the conversation is going to lead, but it's usually not anywhere pleasant. My standard response is, "I'm from the south of Canada." This is both geographically accurate and confusing enough to satisfy 90% of interrogators. On this particular afternoon however, for some reason unknown to me, I ignored the fact that potential hostiles completely surrounded and outnumbered me and incautiously answered, "Yes, I am." This had the effect of riveting the attention of over twenty Egyptian youth directly upon me. If I'd had room to move, I would've kicked myself.

"Can we ask you some questions?" he asked next.

Thinking fast I replied, "Okay, but only if you all agree to the rules beforehand."

"Rules? What rules?

"Simple. First, you must agree that I do not speak for all Americans. My countrymen hardly ever agree on anything, and I speak only for myself." They slowly nodded as they took this in. I went on, "Second, I will be honest in my answers, but this may make you angry. No matter how angry you become, you are not allowed to kill me."

At this there was general laughter and several protested earnestly they had no intention of killing me. I told them, "Good. Then ask your questions."

After some excited chatter in Arabic, the boy next to me, who seemed to be emerging as their spokesman, posed the first question. "What are your thoughts on what the father of Christianity said about Islam?"

This was not starting well. I didn't even understand the first question. So, I replied, "I have no idea who the father of Christianity even is. I don't think there is one."

"No! You do know him. He lives in Rome."

This did clarify things. "Oh, you're talking about the Pope. He's not the father of Christianity. The Christians I know don't even recognize him as their leader."

Undistracted or deterred, the student pressed, "Okay, the Pope. What do you think about what he said about Islam?"

Exactly one year before, during a speech at a German university, Pope Benedict VXI quoted an ancient Byzantine Emperor. The media misinterpreted this quote as linking Islam to violence. Angry protests erupted, and Christians suffered violent reprisals at this perceived insult across the Arab world, including Egypt. On this first anniversary of the outrage, activists made speeches at Helwan University, further fanning the flames. I decided, despite my knowledge of the situation, the wisest course was to play dumb.

"What did he say?"

Another student angrily interjected, "He said Islam was a rash and violent religion! This is a lie!"

"That must've been difficult for Muslims to hear. How did you respond to this lie?"

"Well, we demonstrated in Cairo at the Islamic university." "There were riots around the world." "We fought the police." "We burned their churches." Excited answers came from many of those surrounding me.

"So you proved the Pope's statement correct? That doesn't seem to be a very good strategy."

"What do you mean?"

"The Pope said that Islam was rash and violent." This was not true. He hadn't said that, and he was quoting someone else, but I had to go with the shared misunderstanding of everyone else on the train.

This was my response. "And you reacted by rashly storming out and committing violent actions. I heard in Somalia the mob killed an elderly nun who'd spent her life nursing their children. This hardly makes the case for rationality. I'll tell you what you need to do. The Islamic world needs to hire a really good public relations firm, and then run everything by them before taking action. You blew a wonderful opportunity to respond to the Pope with sorrowful reason and soft words. The Pope would have come off looking like a horrible villain and Islam would have been an immediate media darling."

My unexpected speech drew stunned looks. However they seem to quickly shake it off and fired a follow-up question. "Why do you Christians always . . ."

As soon as I heard "you Christians" I interrupted him. This situation was in danger of reaching a flashpoint at any moment if not checked. Already irritable from Ramadan hunger and thirst, these students were bristling from the campus rally. A mere nudge in the wrong direction could turn things decidedly ugly. "Can I show you something?" Nods all around. "I'll need pencil and paper." Several notebooks and writing implements were quickly shoved in my direction. I opened one to a blank page and slowly drew a large circle. By this point, most of the passengers were pressing in around our bench and trying not to miss a word. I was the absolute center of intense attention. Inside the circle I wrote the words *Kingdom of God* in English. Sadly, I knew the Arabic equivalent but had no idea how to write it.

Kingdom of God

I explained, "This circle represents the Kingdom of God, the *Malekut Allah*—the realm where God rules completely." I went on to ask a series of questions and elicit an answer for each from the Muslim students surrounding me. We established that every kingdom has a king, subjects, and laws or a constitution. For the Kingdom represented by my circle, we agreed the King was *Allah* (Arabic for God), the subjects were those who submitted to and followed the ways of the King, and the laws were contained in the Holy Books. My new friends very helpfully listed the Holy Books without prompting: the Koran, the Gospels, the books of Moses (Torah), the Psalms of David, the Wisdom of Solomon, and the Prophets. I dutifully scribbled these into my circle.

I continued, "It is obvious the only thing that is truly important in this life is to enter this kingdom and live forever under God's rule. This is the only thing I want. The prophet Isa (Jesus) came preaching only the Kingdom of God. He said nothing of Christianity, but invited everyone to enter this kingdom he announced." I noticed a number nodding their heads in agreement. At this time three guys pushed through the crowd and positioned themselves as close as they could to me. All three were dressed in lightweight white cotton ankle-length robes and had the wiry black beards and bruised calloused foreheads that were as much as a uniform for the Muslim Brotherhood. Their presence seemed to inject a real element of danger to the situation, but especially to me. These guys had not pledged to obey my rules. Having no escape, I resolved that if this were the last group I would ever teach, I would do it well.

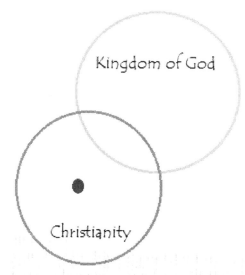

"But I was not born in this circle. No one is born into the Kingdom of God. One must enter this kingdom by the means God provides. I was born in a different circle. Let me show you." I drew a second intersecting circle and inside it wrote *Christianity*. I explained,

"Maybe you've heard of my circle. It's a major world religion with billions of adherents. Many, many Christians are not subject to the King and His ways. I was born into this circle (I added a dot to represent me), but as you can see that did not put me in the Kingdom of God. But under the authority of the King is the only place I ever want to be!" I drew an arrow into where the two circles overlapped and put another dot there.

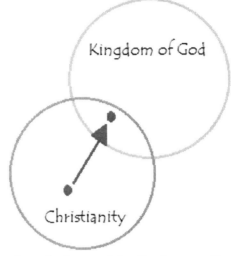

By now the coarse beard of one of the fundamentalists was tickling my ear. I decided involving him at this point would serve two purposes. Forcing him to move would relieve the irritation caused by his invasion of my personal space, and it would transfer the potential for insult inherent in the next step from me to him. I turned and looked at this, to me at least, frightening character. Black eyes stared back at me. I held up the pencil and asked, "Would you add the circle of Islam to my drawing?" He took the pencil and nodded solemnly, so I passed him the notebook as well. With every eye on him, he carefully added a circle beside the one I'd drawn for Christianity, writing in the word *Islam*. Finishing, he handed the paper and pencil back to me.

Seeing the overlap he'd made between Islam and God's Kingdom was much smaller than I'd allowed Christianity, I protested, "Shouldn't we move your circle in closer?"

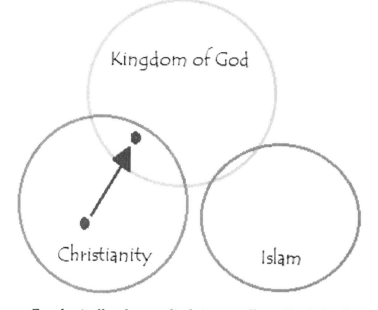

Emphatically, he replied in excellent English, "No. None of these (and he waved his hand indicating the students filling the carriage) are really submitted to the ways of *Allah*. The only reason they observe the fast or go to mosque is because we are watching. If they were in your country they would throw off all restraint." Many of the students hung their heads in shame at his words. He jabbed the drawing with his forefinger right in the tiny space where he'd allowed Islam and the Kingdom of God to intersect. "This is where I want to be. This man is right," he told the assembled crowd, "the Kingdom of God is the only thing that matters." I was amazed to see absolutely every head in the train nodding enthusiastically at his statement.

"*Habibie* (friend), we are completely in agreement. The Kingdom of God forms common ground where we can meet and live under His rule and authority. The last thing in the world I want is for you to leave your circle and come over here to enter my circle." As I spoke I drew an arrow from Islam to Christianity. "That would be shameful, stupid and useless. Even if you converted you'd still be outside God's Kingdom." I put an *X* on the line I'd just drawn. Everyone reacted enthusiastically to this rejection of religious conversion. I followed up by asking my Islamic fundamentalist friend, "Should I leave my circle and come over to enter yours?"

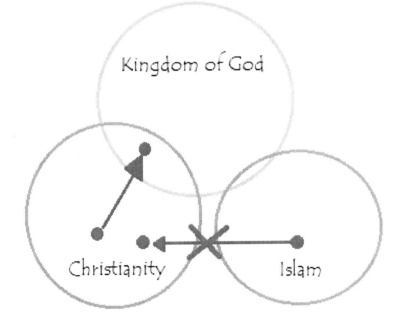

He emphatically shook his head in negation and told me, "No. That would be stupid. The *Malekut Allah* is all that matters. We both need—we all need—to go straight there." At this everyone broke into wide smiles. It was evident all of us were on the same page, maybe not about everything, but on this one important fact. I told them all, "Then we can study the Holy Books and search them for what God says about entering this Kingdom."

As I said this, the train pulled to a stop in Sadat station. I returned the paper and pencil to their owners and stood to disembark. Several students scribbled email addresses on scraps of paper and tucked them into my shirt pocket (alas, all proved illegible) and invited correspondence. Enough passengers exited that I was able to make it to the door without undue difficulty. I was joyfully praising God as I bounced up the stairs to Tahrir Square. He had rescued me from atop a figurative keg of dynamite and created a redemptive encounter that left none of us unchanged. Despite getting no rest on the journey, I felt completely reinvigorated and ready to plunge into the wonders of ancient Egypt.

Y

Y is for Yosemite
(Winter 1980)

...full of God's thoughts, a place of peace and safety amid the most exalted grandeur and enthusiastic action, a new song, a place of beginnings abounding in first lessons of life, mountain building, eternal, invincible, unbreakable order; with sermons in stone, storms, trees, flowers, and animals brimful with humanity.

—John Muir

I love Yosemite. Even though this slice of heaven on earth has made several attempts on my life, I freely and completely forgive and absolve this amazing National Park. In Yosemite, coming close to death just makes life that much sweeter. Apart from my close encounter with a bear (recounted in *B is for Bear*), I came perilously close to checking out on two other occasions in Yosemite. If you've got to leave this world, you could hardly pick a more beautiful place to do it.

Every January the science classes at Crescenta Valley High School made annual pilgrimage to Yosemite National Park. We were shepherded in this weeklong adventure by the Yosemite Institute (Y.I), a group of young and enthusiastic natural scientists and wilderness guides. On this trip, my second, our group first spent several days in Yosemite Valley itself, then Y.I. staff took us up to the high country for a winter wilderness experience. Up over the valley rim, deep snow covered the trails and roads, so we either skied or snow shoed to access the natural world we were there to study.

A thick blanket of snow dampened all sound. We moved through a silent white world that gave every evidence we were the first to lay eyes on its pristine virginity. Cross-country skiing was a new experience for me. Although I was not inclined to sport, I enjoyed cross-country's noncompetitive nature and the opportunity to be alone with my thoughts in a sensory-rich visual environment. My favorite trail was the Tioga Pass Road. When the spring melt came, Tioga would revert to its function as a highway across the backcountry, but in the winter, low demand and budgetary concerns meant the snow went unplowed. This provided a wide and wonderfully graded cross-country skiing trail where one could ski for miles with no fear of becoming lost in the wilderness.

It was late on a sun-drenched morning when ten students, our science teacher and his wife, and our Y.I. guide Jerome—a young bearded mountain man—set out for the Tioga Pass Road. The Yosemite Institute staff had run into difficulty cooking breakfast in the more rustic facilities of

220 | Y IS FOR YOSEMITE

the backcountry lodge, and though their final product was well worth waiting for, we got a late start. Getting everyone fitted for skis and special shoes that clipped into the skis didn't speed up departure at all. Our outward journey, once we reached the road, was uphill all the way. The surface snow was slightly slushy due to sun so warm we were soon down to our T-shirts, but if anything, this seemed to make for easier maneuvering: a boon for novice skiers. Our instructors provided some observational assignments regarding the natural wonders around us. They also asked us to contemplate a topic philosophical or spiritual: I can't remember what. So there was no talk on the hour and a half journey up the road. Normally, this would have annoyed the heck out of me, but silence felt absolutely perfect in this setting.

In the early afternoon, our guide gathered us in a small picnic area just off the road. We took up our skis and pulled lunch out of our daypacks. I remember eating summer sausage sliced by a Swiss Army knife, apples and dried apricots, and handfuls of *gorp* (Good Old Raisins and Peanuts—which everyone seems to call trail mix now). Strenuous exertion and mountain air form a delicious sauce for any food no matter how humble. After lunch, Jerome gave a nature talk, and the group discussed everything from our individual meditations fit for public consumption. The level of openness was amazing for kids who had to go to school together upon our return to civilization. All too soon, it was time to get back on our skis and head back down to the lodge. Jerome suggested a *space ski* in which we'd leave the picnic area individually at five minutes intervals. On the Tioga Pass Road, getting lost was far less a concern than slamming into each other as we sped downhill. Jerome pitched the solitude while skiing as another opportunity to meditate.

I was chaffing at the bit to get going, but had to wait for 25 minutes while five others took their staggered leave from the picnic area. By the time my turn came, the sun had gone completely behind the clouds and sweaters had gone back on. When our science teacher, Mr. Abarta, called my name, I pushed off with my poles and began to glide almost effortlessly down the road.

About halfway down, I noticed the snow was no longer slushy and was forming a crusting of ice on the surface. If anything, this increased my speed and my fun. I was enjoying the chilly breeze in my face and imagining how downhill skiing, a sport I'd never experienced (too dangerous!), must feel somewhat like this. As the snow under my skis continued to harden, I found it very difficult to leave the ruts formed by the skiers ahead of me. I actually had to lift my feet one at a time to change ruts. When I attempted to leave the ruts altogether, I found my skis hard to control as they slid on the frozen surface of the snow. The ruts, having walls to hold my skis in place, were my friends. After struggling through to this conclusion, I embraced the ruts and sped downhill.

I was thoroughly enjoying the speed the frozen snow afforded me, when disaster struck. I was gliding along the tracks left by one of my unseen classmates ahead of me, when the ruts I'd come to trust and rely upon suddenly slanted right over to the edge of the mountain road. My skis followed the tracks before I could even register what was going on. As I plunged over the edge of the Tioga Pass Road, I noticed three things simultaneously. First, a small patch of bright yellow snow provided the rationale for the detour: nature had called and my classmate had answered. I also noticed the hillside below me was incredibly steep. I was going to experience downhill skiing after all. And lastly, I saw Ponderosa and Yellow Pine thickly forested this hillside. My career as a downhill skier (and my existence) was likely to be measured in seconds. The only reaction I could think of was to jab one of my ski poles into the edge of the road in a futile attempt to anchor myself. The handle, strapped to my wrist, immediately punched me in the stomach and knocked the wind out of me. The fiberglass pole shattered as my skis and I hurtled over the edge.

I left the road so quickly I caught air. This is what saved me. Instead of colliding with a tree trunk at high speed, I ended up entangled in the needles and soft branches of a sapling only five yards down the slope. I kind of slithered to a heap at the young tree's base and sank deeply into the virgin snow. Somewhat stunned and yet conscious of my miraculous escape from near certain destruction, I lay motionless for several minutes. I had to remove my skis in order to extricate myself and laboriously climb back up to the road. This wasn't easy to do carrying skis and poles while crab-walking up the steep snowy slope. I'd just secured the pieces of my broken ski pole to my daypack and was beginning to get my skis back on my shoes, when my friend Chris came skiing down the hill. He actually sat down to avoid hitting me. Before he could scold me for screwing up the gaps we were supposed to keep, I showed him what I'd done. Chris laughed so hard the last of my fear adrenaline dissipated, and I joined him in laughing it off.

I let Chris play through, as they say in golf, because I needed to figure out how to ski with only one pole. I settled for something like surf paddling, alternating steadying pushes from side to side. I kept employing various slowing maneuvers, my eagerness for speed greatly diminished. I ended up arriving back at the equipment hut mere moments ahead of the next skier. Chris had already blabbed to those ahead of me about my short solo off-trail expedition, and I endured quite a bit of ribbing as I turned in my skis. The consensus seemed to be my accident-prone nature and general clumsiness trumped snow conditions and unforeseen urinating classmates. I didn't agree, but that's democracy I guess. The Yosemite Institute gal checking in the equipment made some noises about charging me for the broken pole, but nothing ever came of that.

Z is for Zealots

(Summer 2001)

They can hold all the peace talks they want, but there will never be peace in the Middle East. Billions of years from now, when Earth is hurtling toward the Sun and there is nothing left alive on the planet except a few microorganisms, the microorganisms living in the Middle East will be bitter enemies.

—Dave Barry, *25 Things I Have Learned in 50 Years*

State of Israel, September 28, 2000: Jerusalem's Temple Mount, the site of Al-Aqsa Mosque, received a visit from Ariel Sharon and an armed contingent of supporters. Sharon only ascended the Mount after the Palestinian Authority's security chief promised the Israeli Interior Minister such a visit would cause no problems. The next day, following Friday prayers, large riots broke out around the Old City of Jerusalem and soon spread throughout Israel and Palestinian territory. The *Second Intifada* (Palestinian uprising) began.

Jerusalem. August 9, 2001: Hard on the heels of a bitter one year anniversary of Intifada, a year marked by hundreds of causalities and no sign of an end to hostilities, a Palestinian suicide bomber killed fifteen and injured ninety people at the *Sbarro* pizzeria. Hamas claimed responsibility.

2001's body count: 469 Palestinians, 199 Israelis. The month of August's death toll: thirty-seven Palestinians (plus four who chose death by turning themselves into bombs), twenty-eight Israelis, and two foreign tourists. It was a carnage-filled month in a deadly year.

Amnesty International's report on the first year of the *Intifada* states:

> "*The overwhelming majority of cases of unlawful killings and injuries in Israel and the Occupied Territories have been committed by the IDF* (Israeli Defense Force) *using excessive force. In particular, the IDF have used U.S.-supplied helicopters in punitive rocket attacks where there was no imminent danger or used helicopter gunships to carry out extrajudicial*

executions and to fire at targets that resulted in the killing of civilians, including children.... Hamas and Islamic Jihad have frequently placed bombs in public places, usually within Israel, in order to kill and maim large numbers of Israeli civilians in a random manner. Both organizations have fostered a cult of martyrdom and frequently use suicide bombers."

Less than two weeks after the Sbarro bombing, my twelve-year old daughter and I stepped off a flight at Ben Gurion Airport into one of the most treacherous places on our planet.

Strangely, Israel didn't feel dangerous at all. We breezed right through the notoriously heavy airport security gauntlet, and hospitality vans whisked us off toward *Yad HaShmonah*, a serene retreat center chosen by our YWAM Frontier Mission International Leadership Team (IFMLT) for our annual gathering. Our venue was nestled in the Judean hills west of Jerusalem less than a mile from Kiriath-Jearim—the six-decade resting place of the Ark of the Covenant in the house of Abinadab—until King David moved it to a tent in his backyard and opened access to all Israel (2 Sam 6). Founded by Finnish believers in 1971, Yad HaShmonah is a thriving *moshav* (communal settlement) composed of Israeli and Finnish believers in Messiah Jesus.

As we passed through Jerusalem City in the Yad HaSh-monah van, the bombed out shell of Sbarro pizzeria was a

The bombed out shell of Sbarro pizzeria.

brief but chilling visual reminder not all was as it appeared. Ten miles outside the city, our check-in and the excited joy of hugs and introductions to Kingdom friends and coworkers, old and new, drove out any lingering gloom. I was proud and privileged to introduce my daughter into the world and community of her parents' passion. Our IFMLT in-depth tour of the host country, led by our hosting leader and my friend Harry, came before any conference business and took our collective breath away. Harry was not only a decades-long resident of Jerusalem's Old City, he was also a Bible scholar who carried in his head encyclopedic knowledge of every place we saw. As he shared what had occurred in Siloam's Pool, Caesarea Maritime, Megiddo, Capernaum, and dozens of other sites, the scripture he read jumped to life. I understood things about Jesus and others that I'd never even glimpsed before. By the time the tour ended and the meetings be-

gan, we'd bonded as a group and were all momentarily sa-
tiated with tourism. My daughter managed to dodge the
boring adult stuff by spending those sessions with an
American mother and daughter from Kenya. The three of
them had a blast exploring, playing, walking, and shopping with local YWAM staff as guides.

After a week of intense, fruitful, and sometimes ex-
hausting meetings kept tolerable by frequent breaks, glorious Judean hill country views, and hilarious fun—
constantly threatening to break out in this group—we
ended our time with awards and affirmations followed by
an explanation of procedures for safely exiting Israel. This
finale did not work out at all like the organizers planned.
We had all received stacks of informational papers over
the course of the week and had dutifully tucked everything
into the notebooks provided upon registration. Harry announced that because almost all of these papers contained
sensitive and confidential information concerning missionary activity—something the Israeli security apparatus
was keenly interested in and sensitive about—anyone exiting to other countries needed to destroy all of the
handouts. After dealing with some understandable confu-
sion, we all prepared to comply as Harry hauled a trash can
into the center of our circled tables.

What began as an orderly collection, quickly and in
hindsight predictably, escalated into an all-out paper fight.
As we balled up each sheet and shot baskets into the large
waste bin, one brother *accidentally* overshot and nailed a
friend across the room in the head. He returned fire and
within seconds balls of paper were flying in every

direction. Tables were quickly tipped over as barricades, and chaos ensued for the next quarter hour. Enthusiastic participation was around 90%, as only two or three slipped out of the room, probably searching for grown-ups, and our two Korean brethren were absolutely frozen in their chairs; the very picture of uncomprehending shock. By the time it all ended and we pitched in to clean up the mess, almost everyone was experiencing two things: sides aching from laughing so much it hurt to breathe and a deeper sense of really being family than this group, drawn from countries scattered across every continent except Antarctica, had ever experienced. This silly eruption of childlike play was quite possibly the most significant event of the entire gathering.

A visit to the city of Jerusalem was the topic of excited planning and forming of ad hoc tourist teams. Due to its country-wide scope, our Harry-tour of Jerusalem earlier in the week had been light, so we looked forward to a more detailed excursion. My daughter and I were keen to see where Jesus was born, and I knew Bethlehem was very close to Jerusalem, so I loudly asked who else was interested. Mindy, my American friend from Nepal who'd hosted me there the previous year, eagerly asked to join us. She was solo on this trip, having left her husband, Alan, and the kids in their new home in India. Their recent move had drained the travel coffers, but as her region's leader for Frontier Mission, Mindy had felt God's calling to trust Him for the funds and come anyway. The three of us quickly made plans for the following day for a morning exploration of Bethlehem, after which we'd join several others in Jerusalem for lunch and a self-guided walking tour of the Old City.

Our goal in visiting Bethlehem was to see Jesus' birthplace, the Shepherds' field, and Rachel's tomb. Had we thought to consult with Harry, he'd have forbidden us

Oh, Little Town of Bethlehem

from this excursion. Bethlehem was in the Occupied Territories and was a seething cauldron of resentment and hatred. We had no idea we would be among the only tourists they'd received in the year since the Second Intifada had started. Our expectations were more along the lines of the carols we'd grown up singing. Bethlehem was a little town, lying still in a silent and holy night, right?

We got the impression things were not completely normal when our Israeli cabbie deposited us at the check point a few miles from Jerusalem. He told us we'd need to pass through security on foot and catch a Palestinian cab on the Bethlehem side. No wonder he'd brushed off my query about what he'd charge to show us the sights in Bethlehem. Glad we had our passports, we crossed without difficulty and several drivers on the other side quickly accosted us. After some haggling in which a checklist of the sites we wanted to be shown figured prominently, we settled on a middle aged Arab who offered a reasonable price and said we had him and his cab until we'd seen everything we desired and more.

We went first to the Church of the Nativity, after just pulling alongside the Shepherd's Field which, to our amazement, seemed to be contiguous real estate with Boaz's field where the story of Ruth had played out. The Holy Land often makes your Bible stories smaller and more intimate with each other than you'd ever dreamed. Jesus' manger had a church built over it, like just about every other place he'd even sat down. We entered the basilica through a very low door called the *Door of Humility*. Having seen more old churches in a week than we needed in a lifetime, we quickly headed downstairs to the Grotto of the Nativity, an underground cave located beneath the basilica. Our goal was the site where they say Jesus was born. Employing abominable English, a monk pointed out the exact spot, marked beneath an altar by a 14-pointed silver star set into the marble floor and surrounded by silver lamps. Then he confused us by saying the Roman Catholic Jesus had been born under another altar in the Grotto directly behind us. We photographed both just to be safe. My *Lonely Planet Guide* later sorted this out. The Catholic shrine marks the site where traditionally Mary laid the newborn Baby in the manger. So one altar for the delivery bed and another for the bassinet. The most annoying thing for me in the Holy Land is constantly having to imagine away all the religious glop and focus on what happened back when these were far simpler places.

After trooping through a few more shrines and churches, the only one that caught our interest was the Church of the Shepherd Saints. The three of us puzzled how folks back in the day knew to collect the bones of poor despised shepherds. After all, no one would revere them for a couple of centuries. After this, we reminded our driver and guide we still wanted to see Rachel's Tomb. He said we just had to visit his cousin's handicrafts shop on the way. We protested that we were not shopping, had no extra funds, never bought souvenirs, were running late to meet friends, and every other excuse we could manufacture. We may as well have demanded peace in the Middle East for all the good it did us. We were soon sipping tea inside his cousin's otherwise deserted shop while a constant stream of embroidered cloths, carved mother-of-pearl curios, and olive wood crosses and manger scenes were paraded before us. We endured this politely for as long as we could and then began to painstakingly escape from the increasingly desperate merchant who followed us back to our cab. His main selling point evolved down to our being his first customers in months. His cabbie cousin joined in the cajoling, but we were by this point both irritated and adamant, and they sold no *tchotchkes*. Looking back on the incident, I wish I'd recognized an opportunity to obey Jesus in His command to give generously. I can be as typically American as the next guy when it comes to over-pushy sales pitches and so easily forget I have a more important Citizenship.

When we repeated our request to hit Rachel's Tomb before returning to the border road block, our driver truculently refused. I reminded him he had agreed to this in negotiations and again just before the unscheduled souvenir shop stop. After arguing for a while, he finally said he'd drop us off a few blocks away from the site, and we could hoof it if we so chose. We agreed, and not long thereafter we were facing a barbed wire cordon around the tomb. There was no one manning the door, but three Israeli Defense Force soldiers occupied a tall tower on the site. They were cradling their Uzis as they peered down at us. I shouted up, "Can we come in? We've come to visit Rachel's Tomb." Broad grins broke out up above and one young commando, just a lad really, ran down to pull back the coils of razor wire for us. He explained we would be safe inside, but we would also be on our own downstairs, as no curator had come, and he had to return to duty. We agreed to call up when we were through and went on inside.

Once in the shrine itself, we were surprised to see the tomb of Jacob's favorite wife, the mother of Joseph, covered in an embroidered blue velvet mantle and plastic slipcover (like on some elderly folks' parlor furniture). We were all alone with her, somewhat surreal in this fertility shrine usually crowded with praying Jews, and joked we could have had the old dear out for a waltz had we fancied one. There really wasn't much to see, so before long we were out calling the guard. Two of the IDF guys ran down and, super friendly and happy for the diversion, posed for a picture with us before letting us through the barricade.

At Rachel's Tomb with the IDF guards (faces blurred for security).

It didn't even cross my mind such familiarity could make the neighbors want to kill us.

We'd had no warning the Tomb of Rachel was already a major bone of contention. At the end of 2000, when the Second Intifada broke out, the tomb had been under attack for 41 days. Just three months before the three of us went inside, fifty Jews found themselves trapped in there by a firefight between the IDF and Palestinian Authority gunmen.

After walking back to our waiting taxicab, our now visibly sullen driver drove us back to the roadblock into Israel. There were a number of Palestinians waiting to cross the border. Our driver must have called ahead, because a group of about twenty men immediately broke from the line and surrounded the three of us as we exited the back seat of the cab. All traces of the smiling welcome so typical of Arabs had completely disappeared, and a sea of hard, threatening looks took its place. Our driver got out and demanded payment four times what we had agreed upon. I refused, held out the agreed-upon amount, and reminded him we'd made a deal and shaken on it. The Palestinian culture, like all the cultures of the Middle East, fixates on shame and honor. My public mention of our bargain in front of some of the very witnesses who'd watched us make it should have been instantly and completely compelling. However, anger can be similar to drugs and alcohol in its effect on our cultural taboos and moral inhibitions. The driver justified the higher fare by claiming we'd taken too long shopping for souvenirs, and his wait time at the shop was not included in the original fare.

"Of course it wasn't included! We didn't want to stop at your cousin's store. We didn't come here to buy anything. We refused repeatedly. You forced us to go inside. Afterward, you joined your cousin in keeping us there even longer. Your wait time is none of my business—it's entirely on you."

At this, another man, short, bearded and angry, stepped forward and shouted at us, "You are robbing our Palestinian brother! You must give us money!" His stance and gestures were clearly threatening, and the girls both moved closer to me. The crowd tightened around us, and their collective anger radiated against us. I now understood their rage had very little to do with us and was mostly connected to what the nearby checkpoint represented. All of a sudden, an internal message to my spirit told me we had seconds to act before others took the option away from us, perhaps forever.

Two things happened simultaneously. I was compelled to make eye contact with the IDF border guards in the checkpoint five yards away who, clearly aware of our situation, had lifted their machine guns in a ready stance. I instinctively, without looking down and making my intentions obvious, grabbed hands with my daughter and Mindy. The crowd's spokesman began wildly yelling about killing us. Before he could finish, I suddenly and unexpectedly lunged forward and used my chest as a battering ram to crash between him and the man adjacent. Impacting both on the shoulder and spinning them aside, I dragged my daughter and friend through a gap in the mob directly behind the two men. Breaking out of the deadly ring of furious humanity, we flat-out ran for the border crossing. The four Israeli guards all shouldered their guns and began yelling at the crowd in Hebrew and Arabic. A torrent of abusive calls rose up behind us as we ran right through the checkpoint without stopping or presenting papers.

Maybe twenty feet into Israel, I stopped and turned to see if we had any pursuers. I was flooded with relief as I saw the mob immobile and engaged in noisy, heated debate with our armed saviors. Any question of our qualifications for entry into Israel seemed to be a moot point. I wrapped my little girl in a bear hug, holding back tears at how close I'd come to losing her, not to mention Mindy and myself. Then we jumped into the closest taxi, and the driver started toward Jerusalem without discussion. Driver and passengers alike were eager to leave the dangerous and possibly escalating situation and Bethlehem behind us.

If ever a town needed the *Prince of Peace* it is Bethlehem, His birthplace. Always remember to include both Jews and Palestinians as you *pray for the peace of Jerusalem.* Jesus died for all of them, and after 2000 years almost nobody on either side of this conflict realizes what He's offered them.

Our cabbie dropped us outside the walls of Jerusalem. The three of us entered the Old City and hurried to the café where we'd arranged to meet Max and Tina for lunch. The story of our escape from Bethlehem poured out before we even had a table, and we received satisfyingly sympathetic horrified responses from our friends. We had, only the day before, commissioned Tina, one of the most vivacious extroverted women I know, as our new Youth With A Mission International Frontier Mission Leader. I was looking forward to our afternoon of touring Jerusalem together, not out of any desire to talk shop, but because Max and Tina are just plain fun. We'd really connected on the Harry-tour, and they'd mentioned how my additions to Harry's commentary had enhanced the trip for them. This amused me. Most of what I shared I'd memorized from my *Lonely Planet Guide*, though my own knowledge and love of history had added value to my insights. Our group elected me *Holy City* tour guide for the afternoon outing. These explorations would wait until after we polished off our shared kosher repast of lamb shawarma, chickpea falafel, warm pita bread, hummus to dip it all in, and cold fresh pomegranate juice to wash it down.

None of us regretted eating more delicious Middle Eastern food than was strictly good for us, but we left the restaurant determined to walk off as much of the meal as possible. We'd only need hydration, not fuel from this point forward. Our itinerary included the Wailing Wall (the closest we'd get to the Temple Mount, due to *the troubles*), the colonnaded Roman Cardo, and the site of Stephen's martyrdom. Most of the other main sites we'd seen at least briefly on the Harry-tour, though we revisited a few we felt rushed through in the larger group. One attraction I had marked in the guidebook before leaving home was the Ramparts Walk. For a small fee you could walk along on top of Jerusalem's ancient walls. In the 16th century, Suleiman the Magnificent built these massive stone block defenses, pierced by famous gates, in a restoration of previous Crusader Era fortifications. Perhaps the coolest thing about the Ramparts Walk was walking high above the hustle and bustle of the crowded streets below and having a bird's eye view of both the Old City and its immediate surroundings. As I read the description, the group enthusiastically agreed this attraction was a must. Saying, "Follow me to Lions' Gate," I led off. My wife tells me I have an extremely confident walking style and a length of stride that can make it difficult for shorter limbed people to follow me. I had to remind myself to amble slowly enough for the group to stay together as we wove through the crowds and many tantalizing distractions of one of Earth's most fascinating cities.

Next to Lions' Gate, we found the chain-link gated entrance stairway up to the ramparts. Seeing no one around to collect admission fees, I figured there was probably some kind of wall-top tollbooth up above. Grabbing the handle for the gate, I was dismayed to find it solidly locked. We were in the right place at the right time, and a sign on the gate declared "Ramparts Walk. Hours: Sun — Thurs, Sat 9:00 — 16:00; Fri 9:00 — 14:00," followed by some small print about watching your step, not climbing the walls, and entrance being "at your own risk." I announced to the group, "Well, it's 3 o'clock on Saturday, so it's clearly open. Apparently, someone forgot to unlock this gate. Let's walk along toward the next access stairway and stay as close to the bottom of the wall as the street allows." This suggestion made sense to all, and off we went.

The same chain-link fence with the locked gate followed along the street about five feet out from the wall. We'd walked along it for less than a minute when we came across a place where a car had knocked two of the fence poles completely out of the ground, and a portion of the fence was lying flat. Seeing an opportunity to begin our walk at the place on the ramparts where I'd first intended, rather than backtracking or missing that section entirely,

I suggested we go inside the fence at this handy entrance and go back the short distance to the stairway.

Max and my daughter thought this a fine idea, Mindy appeared quietly doubtful, and Tina outright balked. This surprised me greatly because she'd never struck me as a rules keeping sort. Her wandering away from our Harry-tour group on the mound of Megiddo because she didn't fancy the tunnel-stairs down to an underground spring had led to our dear Harry running all over the mound under the hot noonday sun (like a mad dog or Englishman, though Harry's Dutch) calling, "Tina! Tina where are you?" We'd been ribbing Tina about this the entire week since it happened. I responded by presenting my case for how much time and effort this serendipitous entrance was saving us. I also pointed out there was nothing wrong with going up a locked entrance clearly posted as open for business. When her husband indicated he agreed with me, Tina reluctantly followed us across the downed chain-link.

Everything worked exactly as I'd predicted. We were quickly on top of the wall and walking a curving north-ward and westward arc above the Old City. The plan was to walk halfway around Jerusalem and descend at the Da-mascus Gate access point. The views of the Holy City were as sensational as *The Lonely Planet* had promised. We used our map to identify sites inside and on the surrounding hills. I was anxiously anticipating pointing out Golgotha, the Place of the Skull, the rock feature marking the place where the Savior of all mankind bled and died. I knew the clear and memorable view the wall would afford us would be a great photo opportunity and would become a treasured memory. As we progressed, the top of the wall itself was rather less pleasant. Quite apart from being exposed and unshaded in the afternoon heat, it was not receiving even minimal cleaning and maintenance. As we trudged along between chest high walls on either side, we noticed litter that had clearly been up there for quite some time. A balled up piece of newspaper was yellow with age. At several points we had to squeeze past overhanging branches of untrimmed trees. We commented on how weird it was to see a popular tourist attraction in such lamentable condition. From time to time we made eye contact with people in the street below. Without exception, we'd give a friendly wave and they'd stare back in a shocked manner. At first, we chalked it up to the marked contrast between the hospitable and open Arab culture and the rude and standoffish ways of Israeli Jews. However, when we passed a schoolyard soccer game, we were hard-pressed to explain the children's reaction. When we caught their attention and waved, the game skidded to a halt. The ball rolled off in mid-play as both teams froze and stared at us slack-jawed until we moved on out of sight. It was beginning to feel like an episode of *The Twilight Zone.*

After the soccer field experience, the group reevaluated our situation. We had all been coming separately to the conclusion that it seemed just possible they'd closed the ramparts after all. There'd been no signage, but all the other evidence was pointing in that direction. Seeking to alleviate concern, I suggested, "Let's go down the next stairway we come across. I can get us to the Damascus Gate on surface streets." All agreed to this sound plan and picked up the pace. When we came to a stairway we all hurried down and found the gate locked, inside and out. We were trapped on top of Jerusalem's walls. Even in the midst of mounting concern, we still enjoyed stopping and seeing the iconic skull-like cliff at Golgotha. It was so close—just outside the walls and across the road ringing

Our view of Golgotha from the Ramparts.

the Old City—and we overlooked (in both senses of the word) the pointing and staring pedestrians below.

Damascus Gate into Jerusalem's Arab Quarter

We found every exit similarly locked and ended up finishing at Damascus Gate as originally planned. This huge and busy gate, surrounded by bustling crowds buying and selling, eating and drinking, or simply moving through, is in the lively Arab Quarter of Jerusalem. The ramparts widened out on top of the gate, and we were surprised to see a half-circle of piled sandbags enclosing a defensive position backed by the solid stone of the gate's battlements. Whoever constructed this fortification clearly wanted an unobstructed field of fire down the wall in both directions. A single machine gun would turn the Ramparts Walk into a kill-zone. Thankfully, we noted it was unoccupied, and looking into it, we observed signs of recent occupancy: a half-eaten and still moist kosher hot dog, a paperback book, a couple of plastic stadium cushions, and a copy of the current day's *Yedioth Ahronoth* (Latest News) newspaper in Hebrew and English. Tina interrupted our investigation of the deserted military emplacement as she returned from checking the exit—another locked gate.

We were obviously going to need help to get off the ramparts. Looking over the inside of the gate, we scanned the crowded cafés for someone who looked both English-speaking and competent enough to find an authority with a key to the gates. Before we could shout for anyone, we heard someone shouting for us. "Hey! Hey! You guys up there! You need to get off the wall!"

A man standing on the roof of a building below and to the right of our position was frantically waving to get our attention as he called. We all ran over directly adjacent and above where he stood. Now loud talk could replace the yelling. He told us it was dangerous to be up on the wall. When we asked why, he told us the government had closed it a year before because Islamic Jihad and Hamas infiltrators had been using the ramparts as sniper posts to shoot at people below. Clearly an Arab himself, but a citizen of the state of Israel, this man referred to the terrorist organizations with unambiguous disapproval.

We asked him what to do. "Just go down the stairs and let yourself out," he urged. Tina told him about the locked gate, but he didn't believe her. Maybe Max or I would have been more credible to this Muslim man, but in any case, he responded by immediately leaping up onto the low wall surrounding his roof, steadying himself with an upward tilted chain-link fence, and scrambling up to join us atop the ramparts. After embracing Max and me and delivering smiling nods to *our* women, he ran down the stairs to open the gate for us. Very soon, he was back and announced, "It's locked!" eliciting wry smiles all around.

Irrepressibly, he invited us to use his route back down to the roof and assured us we were very welcome to go through his house and down to the street. Other options being few and far between, one by one we climbed down

Escape from the Ramparts

along the fence until Mindy, my daughter, and I stood

with our new friend on his spacious roof. For some reason, quite possibly their eagerness not to be the last ones on the ramparts, Max and Tina duplicated our escape just

Tina and Max make their escape.

to the left and ended up on the roof of a restaurant. Signaling we'd meet up on the street below, we all headed downward.

Along the way, my group had the delightful experience of meeting the man's wife and several of their children. It was remarkable how she hid her surprise at the sudden appearance of pale foreigners coming through her roof, and she managed to ooze welcome and hospitality. I guess to some extent we all fall back on things ingrained in us from childhood when faced with puzzling and inexplicable circumstances for which there is no protocol.

Once on the street, we rejoined Tina and Max and a restaurant owner as they chatted excitedly. He told us everyone was amazed to see someone up there on the gate, other than the IDF soldiers who had around-the-clock shifts up there, since the ramparts had been closed for a year due to fears of snipers. We were the first tourists up on the walls since the Intifada began! Yikes! As we talked, it became clear our survival was a miracle. The soldiers tended to be jumpy and had standing shoot-on-sight orders for anyone atop the wall. No one could believe the post had been empty, several claimed to have seen soldiers up there less than fifteen minutes before, and their shifts handed off one-to-another. It was never supposed to be unoccupied. We assured those listening we served Allah (Arabic for God) and knew him to be a Father who loved us intimately and watched over us every moment. There was no place safer than in His Hands. The faces of the restaurant owner and several standing within earshot broke into wide smiles at this profession, and though several shook their heads good-naturedly, we knew we'd planted a seed and God would look after the growth.

There were still a few things we could've gone to see, but I think we all felt rather more exhausted than just our physical exertions alone could explain. By mutual assent, we decided to go out through the Damascus Gate, passing directly under the scene of our intended demise. We shared a minibus taxi back out to the retreat center. What a day! Whatever doesn't kill you makes for a wonderful story.

Postscript

V is *also* for Vampire

(MARCH 2010)

Note from the Publisher: We apologize for the following story. The author is aware this adventure does not qualify as *Near-Death*. He nevertheless attempted to sneak it past our eagle-eyed editors into the main body of this book. You will note his pathetic attempts to enhance factuality with historic research undertaken well after the events of the story. Editorial cut his draft *V* chapter, and *C is for Crashes* became *V is for Vehicular*. The author, distressed by this deletion, has insisted upon its inclusion in the Back Matter.

Note from the Author: Ignore my Publisher. Okay, vampires are not real, but evil certainly is. The following may not match the *Near-Death* theme perfectly, but it's an interesting adventure and so I include it here. I hope you enjoy it, and that the vampiric subject matter makes this book pop up in teenage girls' search engine results.

In a rural region of Pembrokeshire, Wales, an area that appears bypassed by the last century, there stands an abandoned and deconsecrated stone church. Over a hundred and seventy years old, time has left the church of St. John the Baptist in Slebech to fall gradually into decay. No one driving by would suspect that this decrepit structure, with its broken stained glass windows, has a fascinating and disturbing history. Its story is perhaps of greatest interest to those with a fascination for the world of vampires.

Church of St. John the Baptist in Slebech, Wales

In this context, the naming of the church for a be-headed saint is intriguing. Curiously, the dedication inscription reads: "built to the glory of the de Rutzens and *in memory of God.*" Also eerie and unusual, the church's altar faces east, the wrong direction. Christian tradition demands priest and congregation face East (*ad orientem*), the direction whence Jesus will come again; the main altar, therefore, is traditionally on a church's east side facing westward. Out of guilt for this unholy design oversight, the church's architect hung himself in the bell tower before construction was complete. Beneath the church he had designed and built a crypt unusually large for a small village church. The crypt has a large outdoor entrance opening into an underground corridor running the length of the church. There are seven burial bays, the largest of which is in the center at the end of the corridor. In this tomb rests the builder and owner of the church, Baron de Rutzen, Lord of Slebech.

If ever there were a candidate for a real life Count Dracula, the Baron fits the bill. Charles Frederick Baron de Rutzen was a Polish noble who seduced and married Mary Dorothea Phillips, a young Welsh heiress, and thereby acquired her family estates and holdings in Pembrokeshire. (It was at this same time John Polidori created the image of a vampire portrayed as an aristocratic noble in *The Vampyre*.) The Baron used his wife's inheritance to build and personally oversee a slave trading empire in Jamaica. He became fabulously wealthy through the deaths and sufferings of thousands of human beings. Moving back to Wales after Britain's abolition of the slave trade, this wicked monster, angered by worshipers crossing his land to go to their church, built a replacement church to his own specifications. When local villagers refused to attend the new church (perhaps due to the suicide and other disturbing abnormalities during its construction), the Baron desecrated the old church and tore off its roof. The Bishop hauled the Baron into court for Church Desecration, a serious crime in 1844.

History records little else of the mysterious Baron de Rutzen. The family laid Baron and Baroness to rest under elaborately carved stone slabs in the crypt. Over the years, despite all the damage done to the church above, these graves have remained curiously unscarred. It may also be of interest that the rare Greater Horseshoe Bat breeds there.

My missionary friend Mark and I were not aware of any of this as we drove through the Welsh countryside on our way to St. David's, the westernmost point of Wales. Spying an intriguing old church building with a fence around it, I asked Mark to stop the car so we could check it out. Mark's teenage son elected to stay in the backseat listening to music as his dad and I set out through the wet grass to see mysteries hid in the ruins. Before us stood a neglected yet impressive antique church with stained-glass windows, many of which remained intact. The antiquities board had erected a chain-link fence around the property to discourage vandals—whose handiwork was already evident. However, one section of fence was lying on the ground and allowed easy access. Since we weren't vandals and had no intention of suing the government for misfortunes of our own making, Mark and I decided to go in.

As we walked around the large stone building, peering inside wherever broken glass afforded a look, we discovered no open doors we might use to explore the interior. This was a little disappointing as we could see that many furnishings remained. However, coming around to the northeast end of the church, a tantalizing sight greeted us.

A walkway slanted down to a doorway opening underneath the church. The door was partially open—the first unlocked door we'd seen. Making our way carefully down the slick walkway we opened the door further and peered inside. We could see a corridor where the light from the doorway quickly failed and inky blackness prevailed. Further exploration required a flashlight we didn't have. Both of us were resolutely determined to see something other than just the outside of this building, so we agreed to use the flash on my camera. We crossed the threshold and entered the crypt.

In the light from the doorway, we could see the first two burial bays opening to the left and right of the corridor. Both were empty, devoid of markers or sarcophagi. As we moved forward, the light completely faded to blackness. We would stop, I'd take a picture, and the flash would illuminate everything for a brief moment. Then the two of us would study the picture just taken on the screen of my camera. We proceeded in this manner forward past two more sets of burial bays. These had occupants, and we took pictures of the graves so that we could read the stones later. As we came out of the last burial bay on the left, I took a picture of the corridor ahead of us. When we examined the photo we were surprised to see the corridor ended abruptly in a final bay directly in front of us. There were two large burial monuments filling the bay. We moved closer in the darkness.

For some reason a sense of dread began to grow in both of us. I took several pictures, allowing us to carefully move up to the tombs without falling onto them. Then I took a picture of the inscriptions before us. The two of us looked at the words revealed on my camera screen. I enlarged them so they were readable and we saw that a Baroness and Baron de Rutzen lay before us. I mentioned to Mark that this seemed exactly like something out of a vampire

Inscription from the tomb of the Baron and Baroness

movie and he agreed. Even though I don't believe in vampires, I do have the gift of discernment, and I was feeling that this was an evil place. I had a strong desire to leave quickly. When I told him, Mark said he was feeling the same way. We both turned around and walked quickly toward the light from the doorway in the distance. Coming out into the bright Welsh sunlight and green overgrown grass seemed as if we were merging into a different world from the one of the crypt. Returning to the car, we both talked about the creepy and scary sensation we'd experienced standing in front of the Baron's tomb.

Chronology

The following is a guide for those who prefer to read things in chronological rather than in alphabetical order.

1968 — L is for Lost, W is for Whirlpool, *S is for Seawater: Undertow*

1969 — D is for Demons

1970 — N is for Nail, *V is for Vehicular: Freeway Conflagration*

1971 — K is for Kidnapping

1974 — G is for Gang

1975 — A is for Abyss

1976 — U is for Underground

1978 — B is for Bear, J is for Jerk

1980 — Y is for Yosemite (Ski-Fall), R is for Reckless,
        V is for Vehicular (Moped Crash)

1981 — *Y is for Yosemite: Precipice*, H is for Hitching

1982 — P is for Poison (Philosopher's Plant),
        V is for Vehicular: Cliff Slide

1984 — E is for Exhaustion

1988 — C is for Cliff, *P is for Poison: Death in the Pot*

1996 — S is for Seawater (Riptide)

2000 — *Z is for Zealots: Kathmandu*, Q is for Quackery

2001 — Z is for Zealots

2003 — *S is for Seawater: Mediterranean Slide*

2007 — X is for Xenophobia

2008 — F is for Fugu

2009 — I is for Ice, T is for Tunnel

2010 — O is for Officialdom, Postscript: V is *also* for Vampire

2013 — *P is for Poison: Arachnid Attack*

2014 — M is for Mosquito

Titles in italics are bonus and appear in electronic and audio versions only.

ABOUT THE AUTHOR

BRIAN HOGAN earned his Master's in Ministry from Hope International University in Fullerton, CA specializing in World Christian Foundations. He is a sought after speaker, trainer and coach. Brian serves full time with Church Planting Coaches, a global ministry of Youth With A Mission. He serves YWAM on the Frontier Mission Leadership Team. He enjoys sacred-cow tipping, hanging out, climbing his family tree, reading books, traveling and trying anything new, novel, and different.

Brian has participated in, led, and started organic expressions of Jesus' Body in the USA, Malta, and Mongolia. He coaches those involved in these movements on five continents, especially focusing on unreached and unengaged peoples and where the church isn't.

Brian is the author of *There's a Sheep in my Bathtub: Birth of a Mongolian Church Planting Movement.* These days he and Louise call Northwest Arkansas home.

Brian's Family

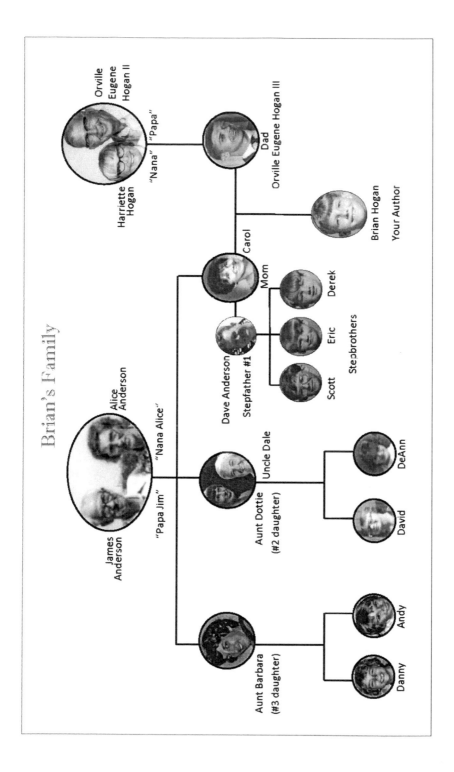

CPSIA information can be obtained
at www.ICGtesting.com
Printed in the USA
FFOW05n1215220816